A Seat at the C-Suite Table

A Seat at the C-Suite Table

Insights From the Leadership Journeys of African American Executives

Charles F. (Chuck) Wallington, PhD

BUSINESS EXPERT PRESS

Leader in applied, concise business books

First published in 2023 by
Business Expert Press, LLC
222 East 46th Street, New York, NY 10017
www.businessexpertpress.com

ISBN-13: 978-1-63742-555-8 (paperback)
ISBN-13: 978-1-63742-556-5 (e-book)

Business Expert Press Public Relations Collection

First edition: 2023

10 9 8 7 6 5 4 3 2 1

This book is dedicated to the 30 African American male executives who entrusted me to share with you the experiences of their leadership journeys. My sincere and heartfelt thanks to each of you. Without your willingness to allow me into your worlds through your individual interviews, I would not have the data that has become the heart of this book. Please know that I admire and respect each of you for your tenacity to become the leaders that you are. My prayer is that God will continue to guide your pathways, showing you what is next in your leadership journeys.

This book is also dedicated to the many African American male executives who, over the years, paved the way for these 30 executives and many others to accomplish their goals. Without your pioneering spirits and your many sacrifices, these 30 executives would not be where they are.

Finally, this book is dedicated to the next generation of African American male executives. Always remember that you come from a history of executives who look like you. In their own ways, each executive has strived to change their working environments so that when you get there, your experiences will be even better. As you are on your journeys, acknowledge the sacrifices of those who have come before you. Build on their experiences, as God shows you what He has in store for you. These 30 executives fully expect you to break through the barriers and become executive leaders and board members of numerous U.S. corporations. The C-suite is waiting for you and your leadership, and these 30 executives and I are cheering you on!

Description

In Their Own Compelling Words

A Seat at the C-Suite Table is an insightful look at the leadership journeys of 30 African American male C-suite executives.

In their own compelling words, executives describe earning and maintaining a seat at the C-suite table. They speak candidly about how the lack of mentors, coaches, and role models impacted—but did not stop them. They talk openly about navigating corporate settings designed years ago by White men. They speak freely about their commitment to supporting the next generation of leaders.

This book was inspired by data suggesting that there is racial and ethnic underrepresentation in corporate leadership roles in the United States. This underrepresentation ranges from the presidency of colleges and universities to the U.S. Senate to corporate boardrooms.

This book provides insights, advice, hope, and inspiration for others. It also includes a road map for all leaders who desire to become better mentors, coaches, sponsors, and allies for current and future underrepresented leaders.

Keywords

executive leadership; executive suite leadership; C-suite leadership; leadership advice from Black corporate executives; barriers to the success of Black corporate executives; Black male leadership experiences; race and leadership; impact of mentors on Black corporate executives; impact of sponsors on Black corporate executives; impact of coaches on Black corporate executives; impact of allies on Black corporate executives

Contents

Acknowledgments

I acknowledge the power of God the Father, the sacrifice of his Son Jesus Christ, and the always present Holy Spirit in my life. Without the Holy Trinity leading and guiding me, I would not be writing the acknowledgments for this book, which is a result of completing of my doctoral journey.

When I returned to graduate school in the fall of 2014 for my master's degree, I had no idea that my academic journey would culminate with the completion of a doctorate in the spring of 2021. About a year and a half into my master's program, on a Saturday morning when I was in the gym on the treadmill, God showed me a vision. The vision was of me in doctoral regalia. A few days later, while I was at work, He deposited into my spirit the topic that has now become the focus of my dissertation, and now this book. I thank God for being with me throughout my life and, in particular, these past several years. I am crystal clear that I would not have completed either of these two advanced degrees, and this book, without His presence and His guidance.

I am also crystal clear that I would not have accomplished anything that I've been blessed to accomplish over the past 24 years without the faithful love, support, and guidance of my beautiful and smart wife Sandra. Not only is Sandra my wife, she also is my closest friend. Her love and our friendship have sustained us, as we have tried to do the things that we believe God wants us to do. Sandra's unique skills as an editor, her ability to find people to help me with academic-related things that aren't my strength, and her unyielding support of me taking time away from her to pursue these two degrees, are worthy of God's praise and thanks. I can't imagine this journey called life without you, Sandra. Love you much!

I also must acknowledge our parents, Frank and Dorothy "Dot" Wallington. Although our father has passed and our mom is battling dementia, I will always be thankful for the loving home they provided for my sister Clara and me. While neither of them had a college degree, they both had a deep appreciation for education. Clara and I always knew that a college education was a *must*. Our parents made huge sacrifices for us to attend college. And, they both got to see and celebrate both their children earning our undergraduate degrees.

In addition to acknowledging Clara, who is an accomplished executive in her own right, I also want to acknowledge the love and support of my other family members and friends. (I will get in trouble if I start writing names. So, I will not.) Thankfully, you know who you are. In your own way, you have supported Sandra and me during this journey. I love you and thank you for being who you are in our lives. I also thank my colleagues and others who have rallied around me and have shown their support.

Since this book originated as the dissertation for my PhD, I must also acknowledge the members of my dissertation committee. They are Dr. Steven Culver (chair), Dr. Rochelle Ford, Dr. Keith Graves, Dr. Shona Morgan, and Dr. Nakeshia Williams. I appreciate the guidance and the support that you provided throughout this process. I admire and respect each of you for your own professional accomplishments. Thank you for being role models of leadership inside and outside of the academy.

In addition, I want to acknowledge four close members of my PhD cohort. Without these four, my doctoral journey would have been much harder. Fortunately, we all clicked very early in our first semester. In doing so, we committed ourselves to each other's successes as well as our own. They are Dr. Shinika McKiever, Dr. Waquiah Ellis, and Dr. Tameka Williams; Thomas Elmore is soon to join us. I thank God for placing these amazing colleagues, and now friends, into my life for this journey.

Finally, I want to acknowledge the many people who connected me with the African American males who participated in this research. When I started this research, I personally knew eight of the executives whom I interviewed. Of the eight, I had phone numbers for five of them. Fortunately, these five immediately accepted my invitation to participate in this study. I also had friends who reconnected me with the remaining three executives whom I knew and had lost contact with over the years. When I connected with these executives, they, too, immediately agreed to be interviewed. That left me with 22 additional executives to identify to meet my goal of 30 to be interviewed. Then, God stepped in and did what God does. Over time, God opened doors for me to share the focus of my research with other people. Some of the people with whom I shared the focus of my research were people I was meeting for the first time. As I discussed my research, these friends, family members, and associates began connecting me with the remaining 22 executives who shared the unique stories of their journeys.

It is on this testimony of God's goodness that I will end these acknowledgments where I started them. I am eternally grateful to God for his abundant blessings, which include the completion of my dissertation, this doctoral journey, and this book. His divine plan for me includes everyone whom I have acknowledged on these pages and the significant roles they have played, and will continue to play, along my life's journey. It is with and through my interactions with each of them that I have found this sacred text to be true: "Be still, and know that I am God" (Psalm 46.10). When I remain still, He works out everything else, including the completion of my dissertation leading to the Doctorate in Leadership Studies from North Carolina Agricultural and Technical State University, and now this book.

CHAPTER 1

What Motivated Me to Write This Book

I was motivated to conduct the research for this book so that I could understand why there are so few African American men in C-suite roles. I wanted to understand their lived experiences. Specifically, what is their journey? What are they experiencing along the way? How are their experiences similar and different from others? What insights do they offer that other leaders can learn from as they hire and groom other African American leaders? Also, what advice do they offer to the next generation of aspiring African American C-suite leaders, especially those who are men?

It is important to note that my motivation to write this book also is rooted in the fact that I am an African American male who has worked for more than 35 years for U.S. corporations. Over the years as my career has progressed, I have often wondered where are the folks who look like me? Why are there so few of African Americans at the executive levels of leadership? What keeps African Americans from being better represented in executive leadership roles?

Before going any further, I want to acknowledge the very important and relevant experiences of African American women in U.S. corporations. Research shows that their experiences are, in many ways, similar to those of African American men.[1] In fact, African American women face

---

[1] P.M. Cobbs and J.L. Turnock. 2003. *Cracking the Corporate Code: The Revealing Success Stories of 32 African American Executives* (New York, NY: American Management Association); M. Harts. 2019. *The Memo: What Women of Color Need to Know to Secure a Seat at the Table* (New York, NY: Seal Press); D.A. Thomas and J.J. Gabarro. 1999. *Breaking Through: The Making of Minority Executives in Corporate America* (Boston: Harvard Business School Press); C. Wheeless. 2021. *You Are Enough: Reclaiming Your Career and Your Life With Purpose, Passion, and Unapologetic Authenticity* (VA: Amplify Publishing).

the majority of the same challenges to advancing their careers as African American men. For the purposes of this book, though, I chose to focus solely on the experiences of African American men in U.S. corporations. Their specific experiences are not as widely researched as the experiences of African American women. My goal with this research—and now this book—is to add to the limited body of knowledge on the leadership journeys of African American males. Equally as important, I hope that this book will inspire hiring leaders in U.S. corporations who are unaware of the differences in the experiences of African American men to champion solutions that will increase the number of underrepresented leaders in their organizations.

My Journey

After graduating with the bachelor's degree from the School of Journalism and Mass Communications at the University of North Carolina at Chapel Hill, I worked for a year as a newspaper reporter in Detroit, Michigan, and Dallas, Texas. Then, I started my career in public relations and corporate communication by working for two global consumer-packaged-goods corporations. I then worked for a global financial services company. Now, I work for a health care organization. Along the way, I have been blessed with increasingly progressive leadership roles that have advanced my career. My advancement did not happen in isolation. Over the years, I have had one or two mentors. (The importance of mentors, sponsors, role models, and allies is discussed in greater detail later in the book.) Fortunately, despite only having two mentors, I have been blessed to have some great sponsors. They believed in me. They saw my potential. They opened doors for me to advance in my career. They gave me assignments that would allow me to think more strategically. I also earned the opportunity to lead other people—a responsibility that I take very seriously. I am abundantly aware that I will only be as successful as the professionals with whom I have the privilege of leading and collaborating with each day.

In 2014, at the age of 52, I decided to pursue a life-long dream of earning the master's degree from the S.I. Newhouse School of Public Communications at Syracuse University. This program allowed me to keep my "day job" while traveling to the campus at the beginning of each semester for my residency. There, my cohort members and I had in-person classes with our professors. We then returned home and completed our classes through weekly online sessions.

Shortly before finishing my master's degree in 2016, God revealed to me that I was to continue my education at the PhD level. I listened, sought my wife Sandra's support, and started the process of applying to the PhD in Leadership Studies program at North Carolina A&T State University in Greensboro, North Carolina, where I live and work.

So, when I finished my master's degree in May 2017 at age 55, I also completed the process for enrollment into this PhD program. I started classes in August 2017. Two years into the PhD program, my career took an unexpected positive turn. By this time, I had been promoted from a vice president to a senior vice president of marketing and communications at the health care system where I work. Although I reported to Terry Akin, who was the chief executive officer (CEO) at the time, I was not a member of the senior executive leadership team. To my surprise and delight, when Terry and I were having my year-end performance discussion in August 2019, he invited me to join the senior executive leadership team. That is when I was promoted to an executive vice president and the chief marketing and communications officer. This invitation opened the door for me to become a C-suite leader. I will always be grateful to Terry for sponsoring me and inviting me to join his senior executive team! With this invitation, I became the first African American to earn a seat at the C-suite table at our organization. Today, I am joined by another African American male executive and an African American female executive. I remain in my role today with the support and encouragement of Dr. Mary Jo Cagle, our current CEO, a leader whom I respect and with whom I also enjoy a rewarding and enriching partnership, along with my other senior executive team colleagues.

Becoming a member of our senior executive leadership team reinforced in me that one of my responsibilities remains to leave the door open for the next generation of African American leaders who also aspire for C-suite roles.

By this time, I also was two years into my journey pursuing PhD. This time in my life was the perfect juxtaposition for conducting research to explore the journeys of other African American males to their C-suite roles. I graduated with my PhD in 2021 at the age of 59. My dissertation research has now been edited into this book.

Methodology

Because I wanted to hear directly from each executive about his lived experiences to the C-suite, I chose to use a qualitative research methodology. According to Creswell,[2] qualitative research methodology allows the researcher to "develop an in-depth exploration of a central phenomenon" through the stories of people who can help understand the central phenomenon (p. 206). In qualitative research, the words shared by the study participants become the data used to assess and understand the broader research phenomenon.

Within qualitative research, *interviewing* can be used as a tool to gather data. According to Klenke,[3] qualitative interviewing

> provides a way of generating empirical data about the social world of informants by asking them to talk about their lives. The strength of qualitative interviewing is the opportunity it provides to collect and rigorously examine narrative accounts of the social worlds of the informants (p. 125).

Further, Lindlof and Taylor (2011) offer that qualitative interviews are "conversations with a purpose" (p. 172).[4] Interviews are

> particularly well suited to understand the social actor's experience, knowledge, and world views. The researcher expects the nature of

---

[2] J.W. Creswell. 2012. *Educational Research: Planning, Conducting and Evaluating Quantitative and Qualitative Research*, 4th ed. (Boston, MA: Pearson).

[3] K. Klenke. 2016. *Qualitative Research in the Study of Leadership*, 2nd ed. (United Kingdom: Emerald Group Publishing Limited).

[4] T.R. Lindlof and B.C. Taylor. 2011. *Qualitative Communication Research Methods*, 3rd ed. (Thousand Oaks, CA: SAGE).

a person's experiences to result in words that only can be uttered by someone who has "been there" (or "is there").[5]

Using this methodology to gather data, I relied on semistructured interviews to hear directly from the 30 African American male executives about their lived experiences in U.S. corporations and about their perceptions regarding factors that shaped them. Throughout this research, I looked for similarities and differences in their experiences. The executives who participated in this study were identified through snowball sampling, a process where people whom you know connect you with those who fit the criteria of your research study (Creswell 2012; Hesse-Biber 2017; Stacks 2015).[6]

The 30 C-Suite Executives

Thanks to the snowball sampling process, I connected with 30 C-suite executives from 12 different industries, who live in 18 different states and the District of Columbia, and who were an average age of 54 years when this research was conducted. Despite their different industries, locations, and ages, the tie that bound them together was their various experiences as African American male executives. Their individual stories provided keen insight into their collective experiences. While each of them acknowledged they have been blessed to have accomplished a lot, they also acknowledged that their accomplishments were not easy. I am forever grateful to each of them for opening their hearts and minds and sharing their personal stories. This book would not have been possible without each of them.

Table 1.1 provides additional details about each executive. Specifically, this table includes each participant's demographics by his pseudonym, age, current title, the industry in which he works, the number

---

[5] Ibid., p. 174.

[6] Creswell (2012) D.W. Stacks. 2015. *Primer of Public Relations Research,* 3rd ed. (New York, NY: The Guilford Press); S.N. Hesse-Biber. 2017. *The Practice of Qualitative Research,* 3rd ed. (Thousand Oaks, CA: SAGE).

of levels he is from the CEO, the number of years he has worked in an executive role, and his educational background.

It is important to note that in addition to age, current title, industry, level from CEO, years in executive role, and educational background reflect their status at the time of each interview.

My hope and prayer are that the stories shared by each executive in this book will pave the way for more enriching and rewarding experiences for the next generation of African American males who aspire for executive leadership roles in U.S. corporations.

Table 1.1 Demographic data of the 30 C-suite executives

Pseudonym	Age	Current Title	Industry	Level(s) from CEO	Years in Executive Role	Highest Degree
Mac	54	Vice President	Human Services	1	11	Bachelor's
Flash	56	Senior Vice President	Health Care	2	22	Master's
Tony	59	Senior Vice President	Financial Services	2	10	Bachelor's
Neil	56	Vice President	Defense	2	8	Master's
Hawk	45	Senior Vice President	Health Care	2	3	Master's
James	52	Executive Vice President	Hospitality	1	25	Bachelor's
Pursley	65	Executive Vice President	Advertising	1	20	Bachelor's
Michael	69	President	Postsecondary Education	0	35	Doctorate
Ranger	51	Chief People Officer	Health Care	1	15	Master's
Chad	44	CEO	Health Care	0	12	Master's
Joseph	63	President of Operations	Consumer Products	1	14	Master's
Todd	55	Vice President	Health Care	0	6	Bachelor's
Andrew	53	Vice President	Commercial Real Estate	1	3	Master's
C1	46	Superintendent	Education	0	3	Doctorate
Blake	66	General Counsel	Higher Education	1	20	Juris Doctorate
Lee	46	CEO	Health Care	0	6	Doctorate

Pseudonym	Age	Current Title	Industry	Level(s) from CEO	Years in Executive Role	Highest Degree
T.H.	53	CEO	Advertising, Marketing, and Digital Communications	0	22	Bachelor's
Vince	61	Vice President	Health Care	1	26	Master's
Mongoose	73	Executive Vice President	Higher Education	1	15	Doctorate
Ron	54	Group President	Financial Services	1	24	Master's
Benjamin	49	Chief Diversity and Corporate Responsibilities Officer	Financial Services	1	15	Master's
John	57	Chief Administrative Officer	Automobile Manufacturing	1	13	Juris Doctorate
Green	69	Chairman	Environmental Law	0	13	Juris Doctorate
Steve	47	Vice President	Higher Education	1	10	Doctorate
Bob	39	Partner	Health Care	2	4	Bachelor's
Derrick	58	Executive Vice President	Financial Services	1	22	Bachelor's
William	56	Executive Vice President	Financial Services	1	20	Bachelor's
Joshua	43	Chief Operating Officer	Health Care	1	10	Master's
Abram	49	Executive Vice President	Aerospace and Defense	1	10	Master's
Al	55	Executive Vice President	Financial Services	1	15	Bachelor's

Key Terms Used in This Book

As you continue reading this book, it is important to clarify the following key terms.

African American or Black: A person with origins in any of the Black racial groups of Africa. This includes people who identify their race as African American or Negro and report their backgrounds as African American, Kenyan, Nigerian, or Haitian.[7]

White: A person with origins in Europe, the Middle East, or North Africa. This includes people who identify their race as White or report backgrounds such as Irish, German, Italian, Lebanese, Arab, Moroccan, or Caucasian.[8]

Minorities: Composed of several different race categories, including Black, American Indian, Asian, Pacific Islander, Other, and of two or more races.[9]

Leadership: An interaction between two or more members of a group involving a structuring or restructuring of the situation and of the perceptions and expectations of the members. Leaders are agents of change whose acts affect other people more than other people's acts affect the members.[10]

U.S. corporation: For the purposes of this study, the term "U.S. corporation" was defined more broadly as public or private businesses in any of the 50 states with at least 100 employees; has an executive or senior leadership team that sets the vision, mission, and strategy for the organization; and the most senior leader ultimately is accountable to a board of directors or a board of trustees for the organization's performance and his or her leadership.

Senior leader: For the purposes of this study, a senior leader was defined as one whose title is vice president, senior vice president, executive vice president, president, or CEO. In addition, the senior leader must be no more than two levels below the CEO on the company's organization chart.

---

[7] U.S. Bureau of Labor Statistics. 2020. *Population Estimates Program.* www.census.gov/quickfacts/fact/note/US/RHI425218.

[8] Ibid.

[9] Ibid.

[10] B.M. Bass. 2008. *The Bass Handbook of Leadership, Theory, Research & Managerial Applications,* 4th ed. (New York, NY: Free Press).

CHAPTER 2

The Problem

There is racial and ethnic underrepresentation in corporate leadership roles in the United States. Broadly speaking, White men are disproportionately represented in the vast majority of all top positions of influence. This representation ranges from the presidency of colleges and universities to the U.S. Senate and boardrooms of U.S. corporations.[1]

In U.S. corporations, White men hold 95.5 percent of board chair positions compared to minority men who hold 3.9 percent. In the CEO role, the next level below the board chair position, data shows that 20 years ago, only one Fortune 500 company was led by a person of color.[2] Since that time, African American males such as Ken Chenault have led companies like American Express; Ursula Burns, an African American woman, has led Xerox.[3]

As those CEOs have retired or have left, they have not been replaced by other African Americans. As recently as 2012, there were six African American CEOs of Fortune 500 companies. As of December 2019, the number had dwindled to three.[4]

---

[1] C.L. Hoyt and S. Simon. 2016. "The Role of Social Dominance Orientation and Patriotism in the Evaluation of Racial Minority and Female Leaders," *Journal of Applied Social Psychology* 46, pp. 518–528.

[2] A. Cook and C.M. Glass. 2014. "Analyzing Promotions of Racial/Ethnic Minority CEOs," *Journal of Managerial Psychology* 35, pp. 440–454.

[3] Ibid.

[4] K.J. Brooks. December 10, 2019. "Why so Many Black Business Professionals Are Missing From the C-suite?" https://cbsnews.com/news/black-professionals-hold-only-3-percent-of-executive-jobs-1-percent-of-ceo-jobs-at-fortune-500-firms-new-report-says/.

U.S. Bureau of Labor Statistics data further underscores the lack of minority representation in leadership roles in U.S. corporations.[5] In 2018, 1,573,000 people reported holding the title of CEO. Of this number, 55,000 or 3.4 percent were African Americans of both genders. White men represented 66.3 percent of the total number of chief executives. By comparison, African American men represented 2.3 percent. Looking specifically at men who are chief executives, White men are 90.6 percent of the total number; African American men are 3.2 percent of the total number.

Looking more broadly at the category of management, professional, and related occupations, the U.S. Bureau of Labor Statistics offers similar findings. In 2018, 62,436,000 people reported working in jobs included in this category. Of this number, 9.5 percent were African American. White men represented 39 percent of the total. By comparison, African American men represented 3.7 percent of the total. While there is a lot of research on the lack of diversity in U.S. corporations, there remains an opportunity to understand why there continues to be a gap in the number of African American males in executive leadership roles in U.S. corporations.[6] To better understand this gap, this research explored the leadership journey of African American male executives in U.S. corporations.

Looking specifically at the lack of diversity in the C-suite, data suggests that U.S. corporations are largely dominated by White men, particularly in the most-senior positions. Overall, African American men lag behind White men and, in some cases, behind African American women

[5] U.S. Bureau of Labor Statistics, U.S. Department of Labor. 2018. "Table 1. Employed and Experienced Unemployment Persons by Detailed Occupation, Sex, Race, and Hispanic or Latino Ethnicity," Annual Average 2018 (Current Population Survey). Data provided via e-mail from Hao Duong, Economist, U.S. Bureau of Labor Statistics.

[6] S. Ospina and F. Foldy. 2009. "A Critical Review of Race and Ethnicity in the Leadership Literature: Surfacing Context, Power and the Collective Dimensions of Leadership," *The Leadership Quarterly* 20, pp. 876–896; K. Ryan, S.A. Haslam, T. Morgenroth, F. Rink, J. Stoker, and K. Peters. 2016. "Getting on Top of the Glass Cliff: Reviewing a Decade of Evidence, Explanations, and Impact," *The Leadership Quarterly* 27, pp. 446–455.

in the labor force.[7] Data also shows that African American professional men are twice as likely to be unemployed as their White counterparts.[8] When they are employed, African American men experience slower rates of promotion than their White counterparts and are more likely to be guided *away* from general management roles with profit and loss accountability. They also tend to earn 25 percent less—particularly at the highest levels of U.S. corporations.[9]

Why Does the Lack of Diversity Exist?

Why does this lack of diversity exist in the C-suite? There is research that offers a number of explanations regarding the underrepresentation of African Americans and other ethnic minorities in leadership positions. Much of the research posits that, historically, African Americans and other ethnic minorities appear to have faced unique challenges along their career journeys that could have hindered their progression.[10] In her research titled "The Marginalization of Black Executives," Sharon M. Collins provides some historical context for the journey of many college-educated African Americans as they tried to enter and advance in the job market.[11] Collins writes that career opportunities for African Americans with a college degree were limited in the decades before the

---

[7] D.M. Clayton, S.E. Moore, and S.D. Jones-Eversley. 2019. "The Impact of Donald Trump's Presidency on the Well-Being of African Americans," *Journal of Black Studies* 50, pp. 707–730; T.H. Cornileus. 2016. "The Brotherhood in Corporate America," *New Directions for Adult and Continuing Education* 150, pp. 83–96. https//doi.org/10.1002/ace.20188; Hoyt and Simon (2016).

[8] Cornileus (2016).

[9] Clayton, Moore, and Jones-Eversley (2019); Cornileus (2016); Hoyt and Simon (2016).

[10] S. Gündemir, A.C. Homan, K.W. de Carsten, and V.V. Mark. 2014. "Think Leader, Think White? Capturing and Weakening an Implicit Pro-White Leadership Bias," *PLoS One* 9. http://dx.doi.org.ncat.idm.oclc.org/10.1371/journal.pone.0083915; C.F. Wallington. 2020. "Barriers, Boarders, Boundaries: Exploring Why There Are so Few African-American Males in the Public Relations Profession," *Public Relations Journal* 12. https://prjournal.instituteforpr.org/.

[11] S.M. Collins. 1989. "The Marginalization of Black Executives," *Social Problems* 36, pp. 317–331.

Civil Rights Era. Prior to the 1960s, in particular, African Americans were relegated to roles in the African American community that catered primarily to African Americans. Those roles included working as preachers, teachers, social workers, physicians, dentists, attorneys, morticians, embalmers, and small business owners.

Over time, though, things began to change. The Civil Rights Era of the 1960s and 1970s brought about different employment opportunities for African Americans. According to Collins:

> In the 1960s and throughout the 1970s, the proportion of Blacks decreased in the professions where they traditionally had been represented (i.e., the segregated professions serving Black clients). In contrast, Blacks increased their visibility in job markets that had been "traditionally closed" to them.[12]

She adds that "although they had been excluded from these jobs previously, Blacks were able to make inroads into high-paying occupations because of different recruitment procedures implemented by major corporations."[13]

During this time, employment opportunities for African American males began to take a different turn. "Employed Black men, in particular, were in greater demand for prestigious occupations in the labor market," according to Collins.[14] She adds that in the 1960s, roughly 7 percent of non-White male college graduates were managers, compared to 18 percent of college-educated White men. From 1960 to 1970, again according to Collins, the proportion of African American male college graduates employed as managers increased two-fold over the 1960 levels. Then, from the 1970s to the 1980s, Collins notes, the number of African American men with executive, administrative, or managerial roles increased each year by twice the rate of White men. At the same time, though, "the net result is more Black managers but negligible gain for Black men in the decision-making strongholds of white corporate America. Despite

---

[12] Ibid. p. 321.

[13] Ibid.

[14] S.M. Collins. 1997. "Black Mobility in White Corporations. Up the Corporate Ladder but Out on a Limb," *Social Problems* 44, pp. 55–67.

gains in entry, African Americans clearly stagnated in their climb up the managerial hierarchy, thereby failing to make inroads into key decision-making positions and in the racial redistribution of power."[15]

More recent research shows that African American males continued to experience challenges. Some of those challenges included perceptions that they were lazy, unmotivated, unemployable, and intellectually inferior to White Americans.[16] African American males are also challenged by organizational structures that are biased toward them based on gender.[17] As a result, these challenges impact the career journey of African American males differently than those of White males.[18] Research,[19] citing research from other scholars,[20] supports this same belief that the experiences of African American males in U.S. corporations are different from the

---

[15] Ibid., p. 55.

[16] A. Ogungbure. 2019. "The Political Economy of Niggerdom: W.E.B. Du Bois and Martin Luther King Jr. On the Racial and Economic Discrimination of Black Males in America," *Journal of Black Studies* 50, pp. 273–297; G.T. Rowan, E. Pernell, and T.A. Akers. 1996. "Gender Role Socialization in African American Men: A Conceptual Framework," *Journal of African American Men* 1, pp. 3–22. https://doi.org/10.1007/BF02733916.

[17] T.J. Dixon. 2008. "Crime News and Racialized Beliefs: Understanding the Relationship Between Local News Viewing and Perceptions of African Americans and Crime," *Journal of Communication* 58, pp. 106–125. https://doi .org/10.1111/j.1460-2466.2007.00376.x; Ogungbure (2019).

[18] T.H. Cornileus. 2013. "I'm a Black Man and I'm Doing This Job Very Well: How African American Professional Men Negotiate the Impact of Racism on Their Career Development," *Journal of African American Studies* 17, pp. 444–454.

[19] J.W. Smith and S.E. Joseph. 2010. "Workplace Challenges in Corporate America: Differences in Black and White," *Equality, Diversity and Inclusion: An International Journal* 29, pp. 743–765. https://doi.org/10.1108/02610151011089500.

[20] I. Browne and I. Kennelly. 1999. "Stereotypes and Realities: Images of Black Women in the Labor Market," *Latinas and African American Women at Work: Race, Gender, and Economic Inequality* (New York, NY: Russell Sage Foundation); T. Calasanti and J.W. Smith. 1998. "A Critical Evaluation of the Experiences of Women and Minority Faculty. Some Implications for Occupational Research," *Current Research on Occupations and Professions* (Greenwich, CT: JAI Press), pp. 239–258; J.W. Smith and T. Calasanti. 2005. "The Influences of Gender, Race and Ethnicity on Workplace Experiences of Institutional and Social Isolation: An Exploratory Study of University Faculty," *Sociological Spectrum* 25, pp. 307–334.

experiences of White males in U.S. corporations. We will delve more into this history later in this book.

The Impact of African American History on Diversity in the C-Suite

The journey to becoming an African American is a long and storied experience that continues to impact and influence how African Americans are viewed by society today, particularly in C-suite roles. Dating back to 1619 when slavery started in the United States, millions of Africans were captured off the coast of their native countries, separated from their families, chained in the bowels of slave ships, and brought to America against their will.[21]

Upon arrival in America, these once-free people were auctioned to the highest bidder and were taken to plantations across the south and were treated as "subhuman and on par with animals on the plantation."[22] These Africans were brought to the United States to till the soil, to grow the crops, to raise the children of their owners, to clean their owners' houses, and otherwise to become a free labor force of White men and women. Since their arrival to the United States, Africans and their decedents have struggled for freedom, equality, and unity in the country that became their new home. They were coerced to a country that had already decided they would be viewed as chattel property, rather than as a human being.

The period of slavery in the United States set up and shaped what is often referred to as the master and slave (Black and human) relationship.[23] It is believed that this "antagonistic relationship" was and is at the heart of African Americans' struggle for civil rights and personhood.[24]

---

[21] W.R. Hinson. 2018. "Land Gains, Land Losses: The Odyssey of African Americans Since Reconstruction," *American Journal of Economics and Sociology* 77, pp. 893–939. https://doi.org/10.1111/ajes.12233.

[22] Ibid., p. 1.

[23] F. Wilderson. 2017. "Blacks and Master/Slave Relation," *Afro-Pessimism Reader* (Minneapolis, MN: Avante-Garde), pp. 15–30.

[24] Ibid.

From Broken Promises to Systems of Disenfranchisement

To further complicate this antagonistic relationship, years later as the Civil War was ending in 1865, Union General William T. Sherman promised the newly freed people that they would receive "40 Acres and a Mule"[25] under the Homestead Act.[26] Unfortunately, for the newly freed slaves, Sherman's promise was rescinded by President Andrew Johnson in 1865. White Americans, on the other hand, received anywhere from 160 to 320 acres each, compared to smaller 40-acre land parcels that some African Americans received. This decision gave White landowners an immediate economic advantage over the newly freed slaves.

Other research offers that since the 17th century, the racial system established in the United States was founded on the belief that Blacks and Whites defined the two ends of the racial continuum. On one end, White culture represented civilized, socially desirable people. On the other end, the Black culture represented uncivilized, socially undesirable people. Other immigrant groups were placed somewhere in the middle.[27]

At the same time, White southerners imposed a system of institutional racial segregation that served to further disenfranchise African Americans. These forms of disenfranchisement included literacy tests, poll taxes, and other efforts to keep African Americans down. "The result was the disenfranchisement of the Blacks of the south and a worldwide attempt to restrict democratic development to White races and to distract them with race hatred against darker races."[28]

Research shows that the White male's "commitment to the exclusion of non-Whites keeps people of color from being fully recognized in either category of animal or man."[29] Parker goes on to offer that "the

---

[25] Ibid.

[26] ASJE Higher Education Report. 2015. *Systemic Racism in Higher Education* (New York, NY: Wiley).

[27] C. Turner and L. Grauerholz. 2017. "Introducing the Invisible Man: Black Male Professionals in Higher Education," *Humboldt Journal of Social Relations* 39, pp. 212–227. www.jstor.org/stable/90007881.

[28] Ogungbure (2019), p. 281.

[29] L. Parker. 2019. "Who Let the Dogs in? Antiblackness, Social Exclusion, and the Question of Who Is Human," *Journal of Black Studies* 50, pp. 367–387.

exclusion of Blacks in America by Whites has been indicative of the deep-embedded state-sanctioned violence, and institutionalized ideology that refuses to recognize Blacks as humans."[30]

The journey of African Americans has impacted this group of people on a number of levels. For example, not only did African Americans suffer from being economically disadvantaged, they also struggled from the impact of slavery to their family structure. Research shows that between 1860 and 1900, most African American families were headed by a female, due to the impact that slavery had on separating many African American men from their families.[31]

Additional research shows that by the 1890s, the "Jim Crow minstrel-show character was being used to describe laws and customs aimed at segregating African Americans and others; intended to restrict social contact between Whites and other groups and to limit the freedom and opportunity of people of color."[32] The disenfranchisement that African Americans have faced over the years continues to impact this group of people. Many scholars agree that centuries of racism and oppression have resulted in a chasm for African Americans and White Americans that has resulted in unresolved relationship dynamics.[33]

African American Men Struggle for a Place, Space, and Voice in Society

The African American's journey to the United States has had a profound and lasting impact on African American men in particular, as they still attempt to find a place, a space, and a voice for themselves. Throughout the history of the United States, records show that African American men

---

[30] Ibid., p. 381.

[31] E.F. Frazier. 1939. *The Negro Family in the United States* (Chicago, IL: University of Chicago Press); Ogungbure (2019).

[32] Smithsonian National Museum of American History. 2012. "Separate Is Not Equal. White Only: Jim Crow in America," (Washington, D.C.), p. 2. https://americanhistory.si.edu/brown/history/1-segregated/white-only-1.html.

[33] L.L. Hunt and M.O. Hunt. 2001. "Race, Region and Religious Involvement: A Comparative Study of Whites and African Americans," *Social Forces* 80, pp. 605–631.

have been "relegated to the margins of society—a place devoid of power and privilege—and have learned to experience and respond to society from this marginalized space."[34]

Scholars such as Thomas and Sillen offered two themes about African Americans that have been a part of social science research on race since the 1840s.[35] The first theme was that African Americans are born with inferior brains and have a limited capacity for mental growth. The second theme was that the African American's personality is abnormal. Research from Brown examined the portrayals of African American males from the 1930s to the 2000s.[36] Four themes emerged: African American males are (1) absent and wandering; (2) impotent and powerless; (3) soulful and adaptive; and (4) endangered and in crisis.

These four themes helped paint a picture of African American males as being powerless, in poverty, and as academic underachievers. Later research specifically about African American males surfaced perceptions of them being viewed as lazy, unmotivated, unemployable, and intellectually inferior.[37] Still other research showed that African American men are seen as being dangerous, cunning, hypersexual deviants requiring surveillance, or "childlike buffoons in need of uplift."[38] As a result of these perceptions, African American men often are viewed as being irresponsible and ineffective family figureheads who endanger the lives of African American mothers and children.[39]

Research also shows that from the end of slavery in 1865 throughout the 1930s, the most common justification for lynching thousands of African American men was that they allegedly had made sexual advances

---

[34] A. Thomas and S. Sillen. 1971. *Racism and Psychiatry* (New York, NY: Carol Publishing Group), p. 213.

[35] Ibid.

[36] A.L. Brown. 2011. "Same Old Stories: The Black Male in Social Science and Educational Literature, 1930s to the Present," *Teachers College Record* 113, pp. 2047–2079.

[37] Ogungbure (2019); Rowan, Pernell, and Akers (1996).

[38] D.R. Brooms and A.R. Perry. 2016. "It's Simply Because We're Black Men: Black Men's Experiences and Responses to the Killing of Black Men," *Journal of Men's Studies* 24, pp. 166–184. https://doi.org/10.1177/1060826516641105.

[39] Ogungbure (2019).

to White women.[40] These perceptions and the resulting actions further emasculated the dreams and goals of African American males. Many perceptions about African American males are also influenced by the media.

Media Reinforce Negative Perceptions

Research from Dixon,[41] Entman,[42] and Romer, Jamieson, and de Coteau[43] (1998) offers that African American men have been misrepresented for years by news media in the United States. In Dixon (2008), for example, it is shown that there are distorted portrayals of African American men as criminals or criminal suspects.[44] A study conducted by Gilens suggested that African Americans are disproportionally represented by the media as poor.[45] A later study by Dixon and Linz offered that African Americans and Latinos were more likely than Whites to be shown as criminals

---

[40] A.A. Fuller. 2004. "What Difference Does Difference Make? Women, Race-Ethnicity, Social Class, and Social Change," *Race, Gender and Class* 11, pp. 1–18.

[41] T.J. Dixon. 2006. "Psychological Reactions to Crime News Portrayals of Black Criminals: Understanding the Moderating Roles of Prior News Viewing and Stereotype Endorsement," *Communication Monographs* 73, pp. 162–187. https://doi.org/10.1080/036377500600690643; T.J. Dixon. 2007. "Black Criminals and White Officers: The Effects of Racially Misrepresenting Law Breakers and Law Defenders on Television News," *Media Psychology* 10, pp. 270–291. https://doi.org/10.1080/15213260701375660; Dixon (2008); T.J. Dixon. 2017. "A Dangerous Distortion of Our Families: Representations of Families, by Race, in News and Opinion Media." https://s3.amazonaws.com/coc-dangerousdisrution/full-report.pdf.

[42] R.M. Entman. 1992. "Blacks in the News: Television, Modern Racism and Cultural Change," *Journalism and Mass Communication Quarterly* 69, pp. 341–361. https://doi.org10.1177/1077-69909206900209; R.M. Entman. 1994. "Representation and Reality in the Portrayal of Blacks on Network Television News," *Journalism and Mass Communication Quarterly* 71, pp. 509–520. https://doi.org10.1177/107769909407100303.

[43] D. Romer, K. Jamieson, and N.J. de Coteau. 1998. "The Treatment of Persons of Color in Local Television News: Ethnic Blame Discourse or Realistic Group Conflict?" *Communication Research* 25, pp. 268–305. https://doi.org/10.1177/009365090825003002.

[44] Dixon (2008).

[45] M. Gilens. 1999. *Why Americans Hate Welfare* (Chicago, IL: University of Chicago).

rather than as police officers.[46] These negative portrayals of African American men by the media precipitates what Entman and Rojecki describe as "White fear and anxiety, as the media connects Black men with criminal issues."[47] Later research offered that the media in the United States is "adept at projecting negative images about Black males in order to sustain the myths that legitimize White supremacy and the racialization of the 'other' in the White racial imaginary."[48]

More recent research suggested that perceptions of African American males, in particular, and African Americans in general, were impacted in the media by former U.S. President Donald Trump.[49] Specifically, according to Goldstein and Hall (2017), "Trump's language, policies, and racially polarizing actions are continuously leveled against African Americans."[50] Further, Trump's presidential actions and public comments threatened African American's constitutional liberties and civil rights.[51]

Crime and Incarceration Data Spotlight Negative Perceptions

Other perceptions of African American males are driven by statistics of them around crime and incarceration. African American men are over-represented in the prison system. Research shows that for all age groups, African American males are arrested and have the highest incarceration rate in state and federal facilities. This rate is 3.8 to 10.5 times higher

---

[46] T.L. Dixon and D. Linz. 2000. "Overrepresentation and Underrepresentation of African Americans and Latinos as Lawbreakers on Television News," *Journal of Communication* 50, pp. 131–154.

[47] R.M. Entman and A. Rojecki. 2000. *The Black Image in the White Mind: Media and Race in America* (Chicago, IL: The University of Chicago Press), p. 75.

[48] Ogungbure (2019), p. 279.

[49] D.M. Goldstein and K. Hall. 2017. "Postelection Surrealism and Nostalgic Racism in the Hands of Donald Trump," *Journal of Ethnographic Theory* 7, pp. 379–406; Clayton, Moore, and Jones-Eversley (2019).

[50] Goldstein and Hall (2017), p. 712.

[51] A.M. Konrad. 2018. "Denial of Racism and the Trump Presidency," *Equality, Diversity and Inclusion: An International Journal* 37, pp. 14–30; B.F. Schaffner, M. MacWilliams, and T. Nteta. 2018. "Understanding White Polarization in the 2016 Vote for President: The Sobering Role of Racism and Sexism," *Political Science Quarterly* 133, pp. 9–34.

than for White men.[52] Also, employers tend to discriminate more against African American men because of the high rates of crime and incarceration among young African American men. These statistics influence employers and, as a result, African American men often are denied job opportunities even when they do not have criminal backgrounds.[53]

The Journey of African Americans to U.S. Corporations

The journey of African Americans to U.S. corporations reflects many of their broader world experiences. After being brought to the United States as slaves, African Americans struggled to find a place for themselves that would allow them to earn a living for themselves and for their families. To do so prior to the 1960s, African Americans were relegated to roles in the African American community that catered primarily to African Americans. Even those with college degrees could only be preachers, teachers, social workers, physicians, dentists, attorneys, morticians, embalmers, and small business owners.[54]

Later, African American males began working in low-paying jobs such as file clerks, mail handlers, messengers and office boys, postal clerks, and sanitation workers. "What this shows is how the emasculation of Black males and economic discrimination against Black males in effect was aimed at destroying the Black family."[55]

Civil Rights Movement Sparks New Opportunities

It was not until the Civil Rights Era that employment opportunities for African Americans began to change.[56] According to Collins, "in the

---

[52] M.L. Teasley, J.H. Schiele, C. Adams, and N.S. Okilwa. 2018. "Trayvon Martin: Racial Profiling, Black Male Stigma, and Social Work Practice," *Social Work* 63, pp. 37–45.

[53] J.T. Curry. 2017. *The Man-Not: Race, Class, Genre, and the Dilemmas of Black Manhood*, (Philadelphia, PA: Temple University Press).

[54] Collins (1989).

[55] Ogungbure (2019), p. 289.

[56] S.W. McElroy and L.T. Andrews, Jr. 2000. "The Black Male and the U.S. Economy," *Annals of the American Academy of Political and Social Science* 569, pp. 160–175; Collins (1989).

1960s and throughout the 1970s, the proportion of Blacks decreased in the professions where they had been represented (i.e., the segregated professions serving Black clients). In contrast, Blacks increased their visibility in job markets that had been 'traditionally closed' to them."[57] She adds that "although they had been excluded from these jobs previously, Blacks were able to make inroads into high-paying occupations because of different recruitment procedures implemented by major corporations."[58] It is during this time that employment opportunities for African American males took a different turn. "Employed Black men, in particular, were in greater demand for prestigious occupations in the labor market."[59]

Starting in the late 1960s and in the following years, African American males began to receive some of the top corporate and government roles.[60] In the corporate arena, in 1967, Harvey C. Russell became the first African American to be named vice president of PepsiCo, Inc.; Reginald Lewis, founded TLC Beatrice International Holdings, Inc., and was viewed as a successful financier; Franklin Raines became the first African American to become chairman and CEO of Fannie Mae, a Fortune 500 company and, at the time, one of the largest nonbank financial services companies in the world[61]; Lloyd Ward was CEO of Maytag; Barry Rand led Avis corporation; Kenneth Chenault led American Express; Richard Parson's led AOL Time Warner; and Stanley O'Neil led Merrill Lynch.[62]

In the government arena, Rodney Slater, was named secretary of transportation; Colin Powell was named chairman of the Joint Chiefs of Staff and later secretary of state; Andrew Young was named U.S. Ambassador to the United Nations; and Roger Ferguson, Jr. was named vice chairman

---

[57] Collins (1989), p. 321.

[58] Ibid., p. 321.

[59] Collins (1997), p. 55

[60] C.D. Newsome. 2013. "Upward Mobility Among African-American Male Executives in Corporate America: A Phenomenological Study," [Doctoral dissertation]. ProQuest database at Bluford Library at www.ncat.edu.

[61] T.H. Cornelius. 2013. "I'm a Black Man and I'm Doing This Job Very Well: How African American Professional Men Negotiate the Impact of Racism on Their Career Development," *Journal of African American Studies* 17, pp. 444–460. https://link.springer.com/article/10.1007/s12111-012-9225-2#citeas.

[62] Newson (2013).

and governor of the U.S. Federal Reserve.[63] Later research showed that African American males have made progress since the 1960s. In fact, 57 percent of adult African American males are middle class or higher, up significantly from 38 percent in 1960. At the same time, the percentage of African American males who are poor has decreased to 18 percent in 2006, down from 41 percent in 1960.[64] This data is consistent with other scholarly research on African American men.[65]

Gaps Still Exist, in Spite of Some Progress

In spite of some progress by African American males, as a race African Americans are still trailing behind their White counterparts. According to the U.S. Office of Personnel Management's federal employee database, in 2017, 63 percent of federal workers were White and about 19 percent were African American.[66] This same research shows that African Americans hold the lowest-paying federal jobs such as bus drivers ($32,000/year), janitors ($24,000/year), home health aides ($22,170/year), amusement and recreation park attendants ($20,160/year), and Transportation Security Administration (TSA) workers ($25,000 to $30,000/year).

In addition, the median household wealth among African Americans is $13,460 and decreasing. By comparison, the median household wealth among White Americans is $142,180 or roughly 10 times greater.

---

[63] McElroy and Andrews, Jr. (2000).

[64] B. Wilcox, W. Wang, and R. Mincy. 2018. "Black Men Making It in America: The Engines of Economic Success for Black Men in America," *Institute of Family Studies.* www.issuelab.org/resource/black-men-making-it-in-america-the-engines-of-economic-success-for-black-men-in-america.html.

[65] D.R. Brooms. 2017. *Being Black, Being Male on Campus: Understanding and Confronting Black Male Collegiate Experiences*, (Albany: State University of New York Press); S.R. Harper. 2015. *Success in These Schools? Visual Counter-narratives of Young Men of Color and Urban High Schools They Attend, Urban Education* 50, pp. 139–169. https://doi.org/10.1177/0042085915569738; T.C. Howard. 2014. *Black Male(d). Peril and Promise in the Education of African American Males,* (New York, NY: Teachers College Press).

[66] Clayton, Moore, and Jones-Eversley (2019).

Projections are that by 2024, African Americans will own 60 to 80 percent *less* than they did 34 years ago, thereby expanding the wealth gap between African Americans and White Americans.[67]

Research also shows that while minorities and women have made progress over the past 50 years in U.S. corporations, these "nontraditional leaders" have more difficulty than Whites and males in obtaining top-level leadership roles from the board room to the halls of Congress.[68] African Americans have made progress in obtaining middle-management positions. Yet, a disproportionate number are unable to move beyond and are stalled in lower-level management roles.[69]

When minorities are stalled at the lower levels of organizations, they do not have an opportunity to demonstrate the skills and abilities required for more senior roles.[70] While African Americans have made progress gaining access to U.S. corporations, as a group their challenges remain. African American males still struggle to thrive and advance to more senior-level roles.

Current State of U.S. Corporations Reflects Today's World

The current state of U.S. corporations reflects the world in which we live. Research shows that White men are disproportionately represented in top positions of influence in the United States. From college and university presidents to the boardrooms of Fortune companies, to the halls of the U.S. Congress, White men are represented higher than any other group. White men hold 95.5 percent of board chair positions compared to 3.9 percent for African American men.[71]

---

[67] Ibid.

[68] Hoyt and Simon (2016), p. 524.

[69] J. Tomkiewicz, O.C. Brenner, and T. Adeyemi-Bello. 1998. "The Impact of Perceptions and Stereotypes on the Managerial Mobility of African Americans," *The Journal of Social Psychology* 138, pp. 88–92; J. Bouie. March 30, 2011. "The Segregated Workplace," *The American Prospect.* https://prospect.org/departments/segregated-workplace/.

[70] Bouie (2011).

[71] Hoyt and Simon (2016).

In politics, White men held 67 percent of the seats in the 2013 U.S. Congress.[72] Research shows that in spite of progress made in the diversity of leaders being hired, minorities are experiencing limited access to promotions and tend to exit organizations at higher rates than White males.[73] As such, "inequalities by sex and race in the most senior ranks of professional service organizations remain rampant."[74] This same research suggests that decision makers, including hiring leaders, tend to hire, evaluate, sponsor, and promote people who look like them and with whom they are most comfortable.[75]

Diversity Brings Some Resentment

As the workplace became more diverse, though, research showed that women and racial minorities faced increased resistance from White men as their historical dominance in the workplace was threatened.[76]

Because White men are in the majority, they get to create the prototype of what leadership looks like from their perspectives.[77] As such, it is difficult for minorities and women to reach elite leadership roles because they do not fit the preconceived notions of American leaders based on masculinity and on being White. This means that "being White is a central component of the leader prototype in America. This White standard contributes to a pro-White leadership bias."[78] Research also shows that most Whites tend to "seek to control White-dominated places, and thus expect conformity from others."[79]

---

[72] Ibid.

[73] K.L. McGinn and K.L. Milkman. 2013. "Looking Up and Looking Out: Career Mobility Effects of Demographic Similarity Among Professionals," *Organization Science* 24, pp. 1041–1060.

[74] Ibid., p. 1041.

[75] Ibid.

[76] Ibid.

[77] Hoyt and Simon (2016).

[78] Ibid., p. 519.

[79] J. Feagin and K. Ducey. 2019. *Racist America: Roots, Current Realities, and Future Reparations*, 4th ed. (New York, NY: Routledge), p. 299.

African American Men Remain the Least Likely to Be Hired, Promoted, and Retained

In spite of the accomplishments of the African American males who were trailblazers in corporate America, African American males today are the least likely to be hired or promoted. They lag behind White men, White women, and then Women of color.[80] Generally speaking, African American professional men are behind their White male counterparts in workforce participation, promotions, and pay.[81] They are also twice as likely to be unemployed as their White counterparts. African American males also earn an estimated 20 percent less than their White male counterparts. The biggest gaps in pay occur at the highest levels of corporate America.[82]

African American males are also confronted with prejudice, negative stereotypes, and oppression because they are both Black and are men.[83] Research also shows that African American men are held back in gaining jobs due to their perceived lack of soft skills such as their ability to interact with and motivate others.[84] According to one researcher, "African American men appear to be on the losing side of a zero-sum game where the progress of one group is achieved at the expense of another."[85]

In spite of the progress made by a handful of African American males, a group African American males remain underrepresented when compared to their White male counterparts in similar roles. Data from earlier in this book reinforces this point. Specifically, U.S. Bureau of Labor

---

[80] R. Parks-Yancey. 2006. "The Effects of Social Group Membership and Social Capital Resources on Careers," *Journal of Black Studies* 36, pp. 515–545.

[81] Cornileus (2013); Ogungbure (2019).

[82] Cornileus (2013); E. Grodsky and D. Pager. 2001. "The Structure of Disadvantage: Individual and Occupational Determinants of the Black-White Wage Gap," *American Sociological Review* 66, pp. 542–567; J.E. Taylor. 2004. *The New Frontier for Black Men: A Shifting View of Senior Leaders in Organizations* [Doctoral Dissertation] (San Francisco Bay, CA: Alliant International University).

[83] Cornileus (2013); A.D. Muta. 2006. *Progressive Black Masculinities* (New York, NY: Taylor & Francis Group).

[84] Cornileus (2013).

[85] R. Stewart. 2007. *The Declining Significance of Black Male Employment: Gendered Racism of Black Men in Corporate America*, paper presented at annual meeting of the American Sociological Association, New York.

Statistics data underscores the lack of minority representation in leadership roles in U.S. corporations. In 2018, 1,573,000 people reported holding the title of CEO. Of this number, 55,000 or 3.4 percent were African Americans of both genders. White men represented 66.3 percent of the total number of chief executives. By comparison, African American men represented 2.3 percent.

As shared earlier in this book, an article in the *Wall Street Journal* by Chen reported that out of the CEOs leading the top 500 companies in the United States, just 1 percent—four—were African American. In this same article, it was reported that African Americans held 3 percent of executive or senior-level roles in companies with more than 100 employees.[86]

More recently, 2021 study by McKinsey & Company titled "Race in the Workplace" reported that there are only three African American CEOs in all of the Fortune 500. Given the fact that African Americans represent 12 percent of the employees in the U.S. private sector overall, the McKinsey & Company research suggested that there should be at least 60 African American CEOs leading Fortune 500 companies.[87] In 2022, however, the number of African American CEOs leading Fortune 500 companies returned to six. Those CEOs are Roz Brewer, Walgreens Boots Alliance; Thasunda Brown Duckett, TIAA (Teachers Insurance and Annuity Association of America); Frank Clyburn, IFF (International Flavors and Fragrances); Marvin Ellison, Lowe's Home Improvements; David Rawlinson, Quarate Retail, Inc., which includes QVC and HSN and online retailer Zulily; and Robert Reffkin, Compass real estate.[88]

Looking more broadly at the category of management, professional, and related occupations, the U.S. Bureau of Labor Statistics offers similar findings. In 2018, 62,436,000 people reported working in jobs included in this category. Of this number, 9.5 percent were African American.

---

[86] Chen (2020).

[87] McKinsey & Company (2021).

[88] P. McGlaufin May 23, 2022. "The Number of Black Fortune 500 CEOs Returns to Record High—Meet 6 Chief Executives," *Fortune.* https://fortune.com/2022/05/23/meet-6-black-ceos-fortune-500-first-black-founder-to-ever-make-list/.

White men represented 39 percent of the total. By comparison, African American men represented 3.7 percent of the total. This data highlights the belief that there remains an opportunity for U.S. corporations to more broadly reflect the communities they serve. This includes providing additional opportunities for African Americans and other minorities to thrive and advance to more senior leadership roles.

CHAPTER 3

The African American Male Leadership Experience

As previously stated, the goal of this research was to hear directly from African American male executives about their leadership journeys and their perceptions about the factors that shaped them. This research looked for similarities and differences in their experiences.

This book is focused on the experiences of 30 African American male executives in U.S. corporations. These executives represent a broad array of corporations and industries. The corporations represented are both for-profit and not-for-profit. The 12 industries represented are automobile manufacturing; aerospace; defense; law; health care; financial services; education; hospitality; advertising, marketing, and digital communications; commercial real estate; and human services.

As shared earlier, qualitative interviewing methodology was used to capture their thoughts. Qualitative interviews are described by some as "conversations with a purpose" and are "particularly well suited to understand the social actor's experience, knowledge and worldviews."[1] Each executive was interviewed separately. The conversations were recorded with their permission, to ensure accuracy. Each participant selected a pseudonym (see Table 1.1), which is used throughout this book to identify him.

Central Research Question and Interview Questions

The central research question for this study was "What is the leadership journey of African American male executives in U.S. corporations?"

---

[1] Lindlof and Taylor (2022), pp. 172, 174.

The following interview questions were used to understand more about this central research question from the lived experiences of each executive:

1. What has your leadership journey been like?
2. What would you like to have more of in your leadership journey?
3. What would you like to have less of in your leadership journey?
4. What barriers, if any, impacted your leadership journey?
5. If you had any barriers, how did you handle them?
6. Are you aware there is a gap in the number of African American male executives in U.S. corporations?
7. What problem or challenge, if any, does this gap have on U.S. corporations?
8. What role do you play, if any, in closing the gap?
9. What advice do you offer to other African American males who aspire to executive leadership roles?

Let us learn more about the executives' experiences as they share their journeys through U.S. corporations.

Q1: What Has Your Leadership Journey Been Like?

I asked each of the 30 executives to start by *describing what their leadership journeys have been like.* Here, the executives vividly talked about their leadership journeys as being everything from rewarding to challenging. Some discussed the challenges of their still-unfulfilled desires to have mentors and role models. Others discussed their lack of opportunities, access, and exposure. The overwhelming majority discussed the challenges of the barriers of bias, racism, and discrimination. They also discussed constantly feeling lonely and alone in settings of people who do not look like them. They described coping with their circumstances in a number of ways.

One of those ways of coping was intentionally making White people feel comfortable being around them. This coping mechanism included intentionally monitoring what they said or did not say, how they dressed, and their nonverbal responses to various situations and circumstances. Their coping mechanisms included everything from being strategic in their actions, being self-confident at all times, and staying grounded in their faith. They also coped by relying on their networks of family, friends, and fraternal and civic organizations for support, encouragement, and a reinforcement of the positive attributes of being an African American male.

These findings highlight that being an African American male continues to have its own unique set of challenges and opportunities. As shared in their own words, the overwhelming majority of the participants acknowledged that in spite of their levels of education, in spite of their career accomplishments, in spite of their awards and accolades, the world still views them as an African American man who constantly has to prove himself and his worth.

In their own words, here is how 30 African American male executives who participated in this study described their leadership journeys.

Challenging

In response to the question of what has your leadership journey been like, the vast majority of the executives described their leadership journeys as being *challenging*. Their challenges ranged from how they are viewed in the eyes of their White counterparts, too often not getting the best assignments and opportunities, to constantly having to prove themselves as capable and competent leaders. In the words of Flash, an executive in the health care industry:

> My journey has been challenging. It's also been character-building; it's tested my values; and it's tested my identity. The most challenging thing has been being recognized and, sometimes, being promoted rests with individuals who normally promote people who look like them. As you're rising, fewer people look like you.

Joshua, an executive in health care, offered this perspective:

> Most African American men would say their journey was tumultuous. And, there were some rocky roads on their path due to multiple things. Race is part of it. As an African American male, you're going into the environment where you're not going to be the majority. You're going to be the outlier—especially if you advance your career to be an executive. You have to have the emotional

fortitude to survive. Never doubt yourself. If you don't know it, you're going to figure it out eventually.

Todd, an executive in the health care industry, offered this perspective:

It's constantly being in a competitive game. It's always being on the playing field, because it doesn't matter if it's in the workplace, in the community, or at home. The Black man, the African American male, is charged to lead. Everyone is looking for direction, looking for that encouragement, looking to be cared for in some form or fashion. So, it's like being on the playing field at all times. It doesn't matter if it's talking to my CEO, my board, all White males, working over the years with females, I always have to be on guard and on the game.

According to William, an executive in financial services:

The journey that a lot of African American leaders go through is that you enter into corporate America hoping to have a shot, hoping to have an opportunity, only to be faced with a number of challenges. With increased levels of responsibility, you continue to face the challenges—be it regarding the color of your skin, your background, your experiences, or the fact that you don't look like the majority. But if you're able to navigate through those, then you continue to gain additional levels of experience and exposure. Ultimately, you get to a position where you're able to not only impact change at a corporate level, but hopefully position you to where you're able to lift others up to navigate through the same things that you've experienced, or, hopefully, to not even experience some of the things you've had to go through.

According to T.H., an executive in the advertising industry:

I think anybody who lives in the United States and they get to the place of CEO, they're going to say it's been complicated. I was very lucky, very blessed that coming out of college I landed with a major newspaper chain. They plucked me out of college and put me in a fast-track management program. So from day one, I knew I was a leader. So, I think I had an unfair advantage. I think I had great training. I had great leaders. I was a young Black man with two or three very powerful White people watching my back. So, there was no way I shouldn't be successful.

For Benjamin, an executive in the financial services industry:

It's been an up-and-down journey. There have been times in my career when I've felt, or knew, I could do more. I felt like I wasn't given the opportunity or the chance to even compete in some cases. Then, there were times when that window would open, where an opportunity might have come my way and I wasn't sure if I was ready for it. But, I knew I had to make that move.

According to Michael, an executive in postsecondary education:

I knew opportunities that I, as a Black man, would receive would not be the same kinds of opportunities as if I were a White person. In higher education, we receive the institutions where they were in the roughest shape and they were heading in the wrong direction. I never anticipated that I would receive an opportunity to lead where the institution was in great shape and someone just gave you the keys and said just keep it moving forward. That's been my career path and that of a number of my colleagues as well.

Rewarding

Also in response to the interview question of what has your leadership journey been like, one executive described his leadership journey as *rewarding*. For Mongoose, an executive in higher education, "It's been unbelievable. I've had highs and I've had horrendous lows. The good news is the highs have actually almost blanked out the lows."

Often Lonely

By comparison, in response to the interview question of what has your leadership journey been like, several participants said it was an *often-lonely experience*, in spite of their accomplishments. James, an executive in the hospitality industry, said:

> As an African American in general and, in particular, as an African American male, it's been lonely. I moved into my first C-suite position when I was 29. It was a Fortune 500 public company. Not only was I the only African American, I was the only African American male. I was also probably 15 or 20 years younger than everyone else on the executive team that reported to the CEO. It's lonely in the sense that you don't have a peer group.

Flash, an executive in the health care industry, simply said this, "As you're rising, having a fewer number of people who look like you." Similarly, Pursley, an executive in the advertising industry, described his thoughts this way:

> I look around when I go to my clients. There's no peers—very few peers. I was with one major Fortune 500 company and it was really unique to have another Black man in the room. After the meeting, we went out and had a beer together. Even though he was the client, we talked about basketball and our families. It was refreshing to have that type of conversation with two people in a leadership role.

According to Ron, an executive in the financial services industry:

> It's hard when you're one of very few because then you end up being the person that others are not used to seeing. You're standing for Black people. You're standing for Black men. It's a burden that you're constantly having to carry not just because you can't be yourself and do your job and do it well, but you know that everything you do is going to be evaluated from the prism of this is how Black people are; how Black men are. That's a lot. I wish I didn't have to deal with that.

Different Rules

Another response to the question of what has your leadership journey been like was that *there are different rules for African American males that have to be figured out*. According to Flash, an executive in the health care industry, "There's no written rules. You have to take the culture you've been given and try to figure out how to craft it into something that will work for your unique situation." Similarly, Andrew, an executive in the commercial real estate industry, said:

> Many African Americans feel that we have to do more to prove our leadership credibility. When it comes to African Americans, there's an assumed level of competence and an assumed level of incompetence. As an African American, there's an assumed level of incompetence coming in until you prove otherwise. Then, for people in the majority, there's often an assumed level of competence—leadership competence—until they prove otherwise. Make no mistake. The starting point is often different.

According to Bob, an executive in the health care industry, "We ascend to a role of leadership much later than our counterparts. Some of it has to do with either the cultural dynamics, unconscious bias, or ability to understand the game and then adapt accordingly."

Twice as Good

In describing their leadership journeys, several participants spoke about *the need to be better* than their White counterparts. From the perspective of Mac, an executive in the human services industry, it looks like this:

> You have to be twice as good as the next person because of the color of your skin. I can't merely be the equivalent or do equivalent work to my counterpart. I have to do twice as much to have a shot. I have to be more of a shining star than them. So, that means I've got to work twice as hard and I don't have as much room for

error. That, within itself, can wear you down both mentally and physically.

Similarly for Ranger, an executive in the health care industry:

I knew I had to be resilient and I knew I had to be twice as good. I know it's an old cliché but at least in some cases I had to be three times better in order to get noticed and to get recognized. But, I also had to taper that with the fact that what if I come across too strong? Then, people are going to view me as the angry Black man. So, the question is how do I balance that?

Benefits of Mentors, Sponsors, Role Models, Coaches, and Allies

In describing their leadership journeys, as a group, the executives acknowledge that *mentors, sponsors, role models, coaches, and allies are critical to the success of most African American male executives.* At the same time, mentors, sponsors, coaches, and allies have been hard to find and hard to keep for many of them. Yet, many of the participants specifically spoke of the benefit of having mentors, sponsors, coaches, and allies at some point during their careers. Regardless of whether they personally had mentors, sponsors, role models, coaches and allies, each spoke of the value of having someone to provide insight, guidance and counsel regarding their respective career journeys. T.H., an executive in the advertising, marketing, and digital communications industry, shares this story regarding his early career interactions with his mentor, a White CEO who led a major business in the city where he worked.

My mentor made sure I was going to be this guy who got every opportunity. So, every month and a half, he and I got in his car and we went out. He would ask me, "What do you want? What are you running into? How are you soaring through that? How are you solving it?" I felt empowered. And, when I got into scuffles or problems, this man intervened and when I made mistakes, this man smacked me upside the head. I never thought for a moment in those five years under his mentorship that I could ever be harmed. If I made mistakes, I knew he wasn't going to save me. But, I knew I had the opportunity to compete.

Similarly, Neil, an executive in the defense industry, said:

I've always been given the tough jobs. High visibility; high risk; high reward. So, I've managed to have the most challenging and demanding opportunities. I've also benefitted from strong mentorship, advocacy, and coaches as well. That's been huge. I didn't know when I was getting it. I had no idea what it was. And, the military is designed that way. But when I reflect and look back and I look at my peers, I can see what the difference was. It was the mentoring and the coaching, the advocacy and the championing when they saw talent.

Al, an executive in the financial services industry, said:

I've been blessed with some good sponsors—and none of them have been African American. They weren't there because the industry just has not had that many. But I've been really blessed with some managers that saw potential and said, "Hey, we'd like for you to do this." Or, "Here's an opportunity." Or, they were willing to put me out there and have me do some things and I knew they were in my corner.

Steve, an executive in the higher education industry, said:

I've gotten support and mentoring and guidance along the way. I have felt a sense of fulfillment. Not all mentors and sponsors are my race and my gender. You take a sponsor and a mentor— someone that's going to invest in you—however you can get it. Don't assume that a sponsor or mentor has to be a person of color. My most recent sponsor is a White female that I did not expect to be my sponsor. It just came out of the blue. She has been a great supporter and has done exactly what a sponsor or mentor does.

Ron, an executive in the financial services industry, offered this perspective:

> You've got to have people—mentors, advisors—to give you advice. Those mentors and advisors are not always higher level than you. One of my best people who gave me advice early on was the secretary of the company. She would tell me, "Come here. This is what you need to do. Or, don't do that. Do you see what just happened yesterday or last week? This is the way you need to handle this. I know you can do better." This was advice from an associate (secretary) who sat there and watched a lot and saw a lot and gave me good advice and encouraged me and motivated me. You just never know where the positivity can come from. She and I are close to this day. That was 20-something years ago. I was a nobody. I was a manager. Nobody reported to me. I was ambitious and hardworking and I wanted a lot. And, she was encouraging me. I'll never forget her.

No Mentors

As stated earlier, several of the participants acknowledged that their leadership journeys have not included *access to mentors, sponsors, coaches, role models, and allies*. According to Mac, an executive in the human services industry:

> There are very few role models or mentors to seek out. Oftentimes, you have to pray about it and make a decision and hope you made the right decision without any guidance from someone who possibly has been down this road before.

According to Abram, an executive in the aerospace and defense industry, "I got used to being the only person of color in the room, which meant that I had to be very focused on excelling without having clear mentors that I could point to in my own background." Similarly, Blake, an executive in the higher education industry, said:

> There has not been that person that has really taken me under their wings to say here's what you can do to develop. I've been

fortunate to be able to be in positions where I've grown and progressed. But, one of the things that I haven't had is someone saying let me tell you what your next steps are.

Green, an executive in the environmental law industry, ended with this thought: "I didn't have someone who could intervene for me." For this reason, Green said he intentionally works with his clients and his young attorneys to decide the work the young attorneys get to handle. "They get a chance to show what they can do. We call that sponsorship."

Q2: What Would You Like to Have More of in Your Leadership Journey?

The following section explores the participants' responses to the question of what would they like to have more of in their leadership journeys.

More Mentors, Sponsors, Coaches, and Allies

When asked what they would like to have more of in their leadership journey, the *desire for mentors, sponsors, coaches, and allies* consistently surfaced for those who have not consistently had these experiences. Flash, an executive in the health care industry, said, "I definitely want more mentorship. I can't find one. I've seen countless others be mentored but I haven't." According to Joshua, also an executive in the health care industry:

> I've never gotten an opportunity from a person who looked like me. Every boss I've had, every person that has ever given me a promotion, never looked like me. As an African American executive, you try not to be disheartened by that.

Joshua goes on to speak about how he observed not having mentors, coaches, and sponsors impacted the careers of some of his graduate school friends. "There were a lot of guys that looked like me that actually got out of the profession of health care because they were jaded by being passed over for promotions, not getting the opportunity to be sponsored in their organization." According to Bob, another executive in the health care industry:

> Naively, when I started my professional career, my thought was that hard work would ultimately result in my success. What I've learned over time is that hard work is, perhaps, the baseline. But it's really the intangible component that gives you the ability to elevate yourself. It's the coaching, the sponsorship that provides an individual with the leadership opportunities for them to be noticed by others and or to have a career path to other leadership opportunities. In hindsight, if I had a bit more of that, it would have helped make for an easier road for me to travel.

Opportunities, Access, and Exposure

Generally speaking, the participants in this study agreed that they would *like to have more opportunities to grow and develop as leaders*—particularly earlier in their lives and in their careers. For several of them, there is a desire to have access and exposure to different people. Several of the executives also wanted different experiences earlier in their lives, as well as now. According to Neil, an executive in the defense industry:

> I wish I had more exposure in my younger years. But, I didn't have the uncles and aunts who were business people and college educated. I'm first generation. They were blue-collar workers punching clocks. No knock on that. They provided the best for me. I dated a girl in college my freshman year. She lived in a part of the city that I didn't even know Blacks lived in. She had a house that I didn't even know Blacks lived in. Her neighbor was the late U.S. Congresswoman Shirley Chisholm. Her Dad was in real estate. He was not college educated but he understood business and real estate. I just wish I had some of those like-minded uncles around me at the time.

According to Derrick, an executive in the financial services industry:

> My uncle who worked in banking and traveled the world was my exposure. My mother worked in lower management in the bank.

My dad was an iron worker. No one was in a leadership position other than my uncle and, unfortunately, he passed away in my freshman year in college. So, I really wasn't exposed to what it means to be an executive in a company. I had heard the terms. I knew what it meant. But to actually talk to somebody who was in those types of roles, I just wasn't exposed to that. In looking back, if I could have changed that, then it probably would have given me an "aha" moment earlier in my life that I would have been able to work into my plan.

Some of the executives spoke about specific assignments or experiences of which they would have appreciated having more. John, an executive in the automobile industry, notes:

> I wish I had more emphasis on finance skills because so much of my job now involves that. But, the reality I've come to accept several jobs ago is I don't have to be an expert in everything. I just have to have people to work for me who are the experts.

According to T.H., an executive in the advertising, marketing, and digital communications industry, "I've spent my entire career until now serving a regional customer base. So, I wish I had more experience on national and international business platforms. I've had to learn that." And, according to Al, an executive in the financial services industry, "I wish I had more experience in understanding technology from a back-end user perspective—all of the terminology, more hands-on experience in terms of putting it all together." By comparison, Steve, an executive in the higher education industry, said:

> I would like to have more experiences working in another state. Many times in the academic world, you go where your job takes you. And, you have to take those opportunities. They're competitive and so rare. Where I've been blessed to get all of my upward mobility and advancement in one system and in one state, which is extremely rare, I wish I had been able to diversify that part of my professional experience.

According to Green, an executive in the environmental law industry:

All I wanted was a chance. I was okay to step into the batter's box with two strikes (being African American and male). Just let me have a bat in my hand. If you're qualified, get in the game and play.

Similarly, Benjamin, an executive in the financial services industry, offers this perspective:

I would like to have more equal access—access to opportunity and (the) ability to compete. I recognize that, in most cases if not all, I was just as qualified if not more so than my contemporaries. I just wasn't allowed the opportunity to compete.

Mongoose, an executive in the higher education industry, went on to note that:

I wanted certain assignments. I wanted certain leadership responsibilities that I was not afforded an opportunity to have because a lot of things were old boy network. So, the process was less objective than I thought it should have been.

For Chad, an executive in the health care industry:

I would like more chances at opportunities that I felt as though I was qualified for. Sometimes when I'm interviewing for positions, whether it's just a phone interview or face-to-face, I never get past that. Then, I go back to see who got the position and I can say I don't think that person was more qualified than me. But, obviously, I don't know what factors played into that person to have been chosen over me. I just want to have a fair shake.

People Who Look Like Me

In response to the question about what would you like to have more of in your leadership journey, along with acknowledging how critical it is to have mentors, sponsors, coaches, and allies, several of the executives also spoke about their *desire to have more peers who look like them and can relate to their leadership journey*. According to Joseph, an executive in the consumer products industry:

> I'd like to have more Black folks. Sometimes it gets tiresome when you look around the room and you're the only Black person there, and you really don't have anybody to talk to. It would be awesome if it was easy to connect to people who are in the very senior leadership roles who are African Americans. I know a few, primarily through my church and through my fraternity. We have great relationships. But, it's not a lot.

Joseph, an executive in the consumer products industry, goes on to share this experience:

> Being an African American at a high, senior leadership role, all eyes are on you. Everybody knows who you are. Everybody knows what you're saying. Everybody's looking at you. Everybody will remember you. I've been in meetings where there's been over 100 people and I haven't seen another person of color. But, when I left that meeting, everybody knew me. But, I sure as heck didn't know who they were. And that's hard. That's heavy lifting. I mean, it really is.

According to Todd, an executive in the health care industry, "I'm the only African American executive in the company. So who do I go to? I have to network outside of my company. It's almost like being on an island." Similarly, William, an executive in the financial services industry, offers this perspective:

> What I'd love to have more of is more people who look like me; more people who have my walk and my experience in positions of authority and in the C-suite so that we could partner together to create avenues for others to be brought up over the course of time.

William went on to say:

Corporate America is a bit of a fraternity to a degree. It's a relationship-built environment. And, typically, relationships are built on commonalities. When you go on executive leadership teams, or you're going to conferences, or you're in big forums or big groups where you're the only one, or you're a handful of one, there's a tendency to not feel like you belong. You don't look like the people you're around. You don't have the experiences like them.

I remember being at dinner one night with about 20 of my peers. And, everyone was talking about their high school experiences. Then, they began talking about their favorite songs. I began to see patterns of songs or artists I'd never heard—or things I wouldn't do. By the time they got around to me, I pretended I had an important phone call. So, I stood up, took the call, and began to walk out of the restaurant and to my hotel room and I got into bed.

You reach this point where you don't have anything in common. You don't feel like you belong. You feel like you are on the outside. The reality is you may have some things in common. But, you really never open yourself up because you just don't feel you belong.

C1, an executive in the education industry, simply says, "I want more individuals who look like me to help pave the way."

Self-Confidence

A few of the participants acknowledged their own *need to be more self-confident* as they progressed in their leadership journeys. Two of the executives spoke specifically about wanting more confidence about expressing themselves in the workplace earlier in their careers. According to Hawk, an executive in the health care industry:

I wish I had more gumption and "umption" to know that you don't have to have a terminal degree to speak up and to weigh in on things, and to give your opinion and to say "no that's not the way it's seen and done in my community. Hear my voice and hear my experience." I've always been a person to speak up. But sometimes, instead of speaking up, I might have shied away.

Similarly, Ron, an executive in the financial services industry, said:

Early on, I held back a lot. I probably shouldn't have. I wish I had more awareness that I didn't need to wear the mask and try to hide my individuality. I wish I had done that sooner in my career. It didn't hurt me. Everything worked out but I should have done that sooner.

Q3: What Would You Like to Have Less of in Your Leadership Journey?

The following section explores the executives' responses to the question of what would you like to have less of in your leadership journeys.

Race, Racism, Conscious, and Unconscious Biases

When asked what they would like to have *less* of in their leadership journeys, *race, racism, conscious, and unconscious biases surfaced for most of the executives.* This theme rose to the top, particularly as these executives discussed what they would like to have less of in their career journeys. It also was the dominant theme when the executives were asked what barriers, if any, impacted their leadership journeys. According to Flash, an executive in the health care industry:

I'd like to have less of people being comfortable in their bias. You probably noticed I didn't say unconscious. I think they were very conscious and I've watched a lot of very conscious winking and nodding. So, they were very well aware. It's not verbalized. But it was very intentional biases. I don't know if I can count the number of opportunities that have not been realized (as a result of bias). I've actually had people tell me they don't have a reason why they won't promote me.

According to Ranger, also an executive in the health care industry:

I would like to have less of the biases that I experienced and I saw firsthand. I've been in meetings where I've noticed that people, present company included, will make a statement and be passionate about it. Then people ask "why are you being so hostile?" Then, I watch a colleague or colleagues who curse and slam and hit the table—and they're just being passionate. Help me understand what is hostile about what I just did and hitting the table and cussing people out is not hostile?

Andrew, an executive in the commercial real estate industry, added this perspective:

I'd like to have less of the unfair scrutiny. It will come in the performance assessment or performance appraisal. When I think of either myself or other African American leaders, when something is not accomplished or done to the extent that it should have been, it's often overly attributed to that individual. And, then, I've noticed that with others, if the individual is the majority, it's often attributed to external factors. It was the business environment. It was a tough economic time. They'll put it everywhere else.

Andrew goes on to say that:

There are biases. When individuals in leadership, or executive leadership who are making decisions, they tend to have a profile—a very narrow profile—of what good looks like, walks like, talks like; what background they come from; what school. And that is a limiting factor on African Americans in leadership. We're different. We're the other. And people are more comfortable with individuals who are more like them. So, that bias, both conscious and unconscious, has a huge factor not only on myself but on others.

According to William, an executive in the financial services industry, "I'd like to have less challenges that are brought on due to things that have absolutely nothing to do with the role that I'm in. They're typically driven by just racial stereotypes."

Being Misunderstood as an African American Man

In response to the question of what they would like to have less of in their leadership journeys, several of the executives cited *being misunderstood as an African American man*. These misunderstandings, from the participants' perspectives, include their physical stature, to how they react to certain situations, to the emotional strain of living in multiple worlds. Mac, an executive in the human services industry, described it this way:

> I would like to have less situations where I felt I was not treated fairly, or not being evaluated fairly, or that there wasn't some form of prejudice about my stature, the color of my skin, my gender—whatever it may be. You could always sense when any of those might be an issue. I would like to not have so much pressure to feel like that. There's also the added weight of making sure that I do everything right so that I don't mess it up for the next person. That's added pressure that I don't enjoy to this day.

Mac also wanted to feel that he could handle various personal situations differently at work with his leader. According to Mac:

> I can remember being sick as a dog. But I went to work because I didn't want to be out sick on a Friday or a Monday. I didn't want the perception to be that I was just looking for a long weekend. I also don't want to feel like if I decide I want to grow a beard or a mustache, that I would be frowned upon because some people see that as being inappropriate in a professional work environment. I want to be able to know that me having a beard isn't a big deal.

According to Bob, "There's always this perception that Black men are always angry or we're intimidating. So, just trying to find ways to make people comfortable with me. A lot of my career has been being agile and adjusting on the fly." Similarly, Hawk shared that:

> I'm 6′3″. I weigh 245 pounds. I'm a big-statured guy and I'm dark skinned. So, it's hard to forget that I'm Black. They sometimes forget because of my sense of creating a safe environment and authentic environment for anybody that's around me. I just think I make people feel comfortable. I then use that to enlighten and to provide feedback from a perspective that I think is needed to balance out the optics.

For Al, an executive in the financial services industry:

> There's always been the sense of needing to be more careful about what I say and how I say it. Also, I have found myself reluctant to do some things because I didn't think I would be well-received in the environment. Wealth Management and Trust was a potential area of interest. Also, commercial banking. How would a commercial customer receive an African American banker? Some of that I had to get over and move on. But, I did consider it a factor. It may have been a self-imposed limitation. But, nonetheless, it was part of how I navigated my career.

To this, Neil, an executive in the defense industry, added:

> As African American men, we can choose to stay very comfortable in the communities we grew up in for the rest of our lives and not have friendships with White people or people of other cultures and not understand the richness of those relationships. But for those of us who do so, it's like living in two worlds, right? From the time I wake up and walk out (of) my door, before I get to work, I'm going to have about two or three different experiences. And, I have to be able to flip, mentally and physically, sometimes from the time I leave my door to the time I get to my office, depending on what happens. This can be exhausting. It's not for everybody. Some (African American) people don't want to put up with it.

Q4: What Barriers, If Any, Impacted Your Leadership Journey?

The following section explores the participants' responses to the question of what barriers, if any, impacted your leadership journey.

Race and Racism

In response to the question of what barriers, if any, impacted your leadership journey, the overwhelming majority of the executives said that *race and racism were present in their experiences*. For them, race and racism were manifested in how their leaders, peers, and team members view them and their ability to lead in environments that were designed by White males for the success of White males. According to Mongoose, an executive in the higher education industry:

> Race is a barrier. I can't state that enough. I had to work out strategies wherein some jobs when I knew the answer, I knew they wouldn't hear it from me. So, I had to whisper to the White guy next to me and he would say the same thing I was saying. But they heard him. So, I just learned how to work that way. I didn't care who got the credit as much as making sure that the mission was accomplished.

Similarly, for John, an executive in the automotive industry:

> A barrier has been there's a perception about Blacks in general, and Black men in particular, in the minds of White peers or White superiors. I've always had to deal with it and battle through it. It varies from person to person. But, for someone my age (57-years old), if you're dealing with a White peer or a White boss, they're coming to you with a set of perceptions about how you should function, how capable you are, what you can do and what you can't. Sometimes they're overt about these perceptions and sometimes they're subtle. If you've been around long enough, you learn to spot them pretty quickly. Early in my career, I thought it was my job to completely blow apart those perceptions and demonstrate my superiority to them. Lately, as I've gotten older

and more mature, I've decided the best way to deal with them is to just be myself and not spend a lot of time thinking about or worrying about how others' perceptions about me being a Black man. I won't allow that to obstruct what I'm put on the planet to do.

For Blake, an executive in the higher education industry, "Part of the barrier is that (White) people don't see us in positions like this. It's not even a glass ceiling because I think they cover it up so you don't see what's up there."

Lee, an executive in the health care industry, offers this perspective:

My barrier is that I have to hide my identity. There's certain things I can't bring into my office. People will say, "Who do you think you are? You must think you're somebody." That's the way you end up on the bottom. So keep your head down and grind it out.

Derrick, an executive in the financial services industry, says:

White America has their own definition around what success looks like. As I advance my career, you start to see and hear things where certain words would be used to describe women and African Americans. "Wow. They're pretty aggressive." Or, "She's so assertive." It would be used in a context of that's a bad thing. But when they describe the White person, it would be more about, "They're very confident. They have a can-do attitude."

Green, an executive in the environmental law industry, adds this perspective, noting that:

I'll get that look where people are looking for the person who is the leader in the room. Even if they know who I am, sometimes they have a demeaning tone or attitude. That's when I get my game face on. The truth is that race is there. It's always there. But I try not to use it as a justification for the answer to success. I try to use that as fuel to propel me.

According to Benjamin, an executive in the financial services industry, "The success of your leadership is not just you. It's the system, or your peers or counterparts." He goes on to say that:

> In terms of leading people, I've definitely had instances where people have had a problem reporting to me—probably as a Black person and especially earlier in my career as a Black person who was and sometimes looks very young. Also, when I used to travel globally, there were times I would travel with White subordinates. And, it was assumed that I was the subordinate and that the White person was my leader. There are plenty of times when, even if they know you're the leader, that they defer to someone else in the room. As Black executives, we learn to manage those situations.

Ron, an executive in the financial services industry, offers this perspective on barriers when he reflects on what his leadership journey could be like if he were a White man:

> I can't even imagine what it's like being a White man. I don't want to be a White man. But by being a White man, you always get the benefit of the doubt. You don't get second guessed. I just can't even imagine what that life is like. I'm not worried about it. I'm not changing my life. I'm just saying they have no idea the privilege they live with. Everywhere you go you're just assumed that you can pay for it, assumed that you're in the right, assumed that you're probably qualified—even when you may not be. Just a lot of positive assumptions made. You're given the benefit of the doubt. Whereas, when you're a Black male in America, most of the time you're overcoming someone's biases or questions or concerns. I just can't imagine not having to deal with that.

Q5: If You Had Any Barriers, How Did You Overcome Them?

The following sections explore how the executives responded to the question of if you had any barriers, how did you overcome them.

Faith, Family, Colleagues, and Fraternities

When asked if they had any barriers how they overcame them, a significant number of the executives said *their faith, families, friends, fraternities, and other organizations and networks provide critical support in dealing with barriers in their leadership journeys*, making this a dominant theme. As it pertains specifically to faith, William, an executive in the financial services industry, said:

> There's things and experiences that are bigger than me. And, there's a walk and a purpose that I have in my life. In order to get to some things, you're going to have to go through some things. If I quit in the face of a barrier, then I would feel like I'm not creating the opportunity for others who looked like me—or who had similar experiences—to benefit from my experiences.

According to Al, an executive in the financial services industry:

> I'm a man of faith. I have found that to be very grounding and motivating. It's created some good perspective for me to appreciate that my professional life—and how I may be perceived—is not the sum total of my being. That has been liberating in many ways. I don't feel like what I accomplish in my professional career is all there is.

According to Lee, an executive in the health care industry, "I'm a man of faith. So, I believe everything happens for a reason. And, I believe that God sets things in your path to prepare you for the next level." Similarly, Vince, also an executive in the health care industry, said:

> When I have barriers, I'm a big believer in God. I have a lot of faith. I was brought up in the church. I've always had people that I felt I could go to who've always provided me with great guidance.

Several of the executives spoke about the support of family, colleagues, and fraternities. According to James, an executive in the hospitality industry, "There was a lot of consensus building and discussion with people I trust in my inner circle—my wife, my family, my parents, and siblings. And, recognizing that this, too, whatever it is, shall pass." Similarly, Bob, an executive in the health care industry, said, "My upbringing and my parents gave me the foundation in order for me to survive in this environment. Also, I've learned to take every experience and learn from it and adjust accordingly to not make the same mistake again."

According to Joseph, an executive in the consumer products industry:

I had a HR partner that I was able to confide in. That really helped me work through a very, very difficult situation. I never brought work home. I guess I've been fortunate enough where I've been able to keep it at the office—even when I'm struggling, even when there's difficult times. I've always tried to keep that stuff away from my wife and the kids. I don't want them to worry about stuff like that. So that's what helped me get through the challenging times—having someone to lean on and talk to and get advice. If you don't have that, you just can't survive in corporate America. You cannot survive just on your technical skills. It's not going to work. It'll kill you.

T.H., an executive in the advertising, marketing, and digital communications industry, noted that:

You have to have key White colleagues or advocates. You really do need to connect and find colleagues and advocates and partners who don't look like you who are committed to your success. You have to be able to balance your frustrations with reality—in confidence. That's what having those relationships can do for you.

Similarly, Abram, an executive in the aerospace and defense industry, offered these thoughts:

I built allyship with someone who believed in me that had the ear of the CEO. By getting him to buy into the vision, and then laying out for him how we would take what I was doing and have it still address a problem that he (the CEO) was trying to solve for, that was the connection. As you move up in these executive roles, you've got to be focused on creating that linkage between what the CEO wants and the board wants and then what you want to do to support them.

As it pertains specifically to fraternities, Mac, an executive in the human services industry, explains that:

Fraternities are important because they become a sounding board for day-to-day issues—both personally and professionally. Many of them serve as inspiration and motivation for continued achievement. Fraternities provide someone who shares some of the same experiences that you're having—who can identify with what you're saying.

Similarly, T.H., an executive in the advertising, marketing, and digital communications industry, shares this thought:

You've got to have a support system that allows you to talk freely and in a safe place about your frustrations. So, for me, I'm a member of an organization where I can sit down with two or three (African American) brothers in a safe space and talk freely.

Todd, an executive in the health care industry, simply said, "Networks are essential. Being able to get into organizations is just as essential. Sharing thoughts and ideas with others extends me beyond what I do on a regular basis."

Being Strategic and Being Persistent

Several of the executives spoke of overcoming barriers by *anticipating challenges, being self-confident, and handling challenging situations head-on.* According to Flash, an executive in the health care industry:

Strategize your way through it and accept the challenges that you know others don't have to deal with. You're going to have to sacrifice and you're going to have to have your family sacrifice with you. You're probably going to have to uproot more than you want to. You might have to go places you really don't want to be. You may even have to give up some compensation to get a title, or at least a reputation or a brand of a title.

According to Neil, an executive in the defense industry, "My military training has allowed me to work through challenges by being a strategic-minded thinker, to maneuver through organizations, to understand the potholes and the trapdoors." Similarly, Green, an executive in the environmental law industry, said, "I anticipated the barriers would be there. It never occurred to me it would be fair. I expect to be tough enough to survive and good enough to overcome the unfairness of the situation." John, an executive in the automobile manufacturing industry, offered this perspective:

It's important to understand people's mindsets when they deal with you, when they approach you—particularly when you're dealing with a predominately White power structure. So, you have to figure out who are the people who just can't process you from day one—because they think you're inferior or they just don't like Black people, or they can't imagine that you're swimming in the same pool that they're swimming in. And, they react accordingly. One way I get around it is to figure out who these people are. They usually will give you some pretty strong indicators—if you learn to know what to look for. Then, you manage around them or through them or over them. And, don't spend a lot of time trying to change their mind. That's not your job. Your job is to function effectively.

According to Tony, an executive in the financial services industry:

I'm persistent and I never give up. I never allowed myself to settle and just bow out of the competition. Being the competitive person that I am, I was up to the challenge. I was raised to pursue my goals and by any means necessary, within reason. So I think it was my pure determination and persistence that allowed me to stay in the game. And, if there was an obstacle in the front door, I would go in through the back door. If there was an opportunity that was evading me, I would simply try to apply some other strategy to achieve the same goal.

Joshua, an executive in the health care industry, added that "You have to have the emotional fortitude. I never doubted myself, even though I might not have known everything at the time. I never doubted. If you don't know it, you're going to figure it out eventually." Al, an executive in the financial services industry, expanded on this theme:

I'm going to work hard and know my stuff. I'm going to play to my strengths and make a decision based on competence. I'm going to embrace the moment and be willing to step out there and do what I know I'm capable of.

William, also an executive in the financial services industry, shared that he was "brought up to fight for what is right, to fight for what you believe in, and to be the very best that you can be." Similarly, according to Derrick, who is also an executive in the financial services industry, "When I did run into barriers, I would just confront them. I know it put people on the defense. But, I've always been taught to seek understanding." For Pursley, an executive in the advertising industry:

I addressed them (barriers) directly in different ways. I would address the situation, whether it was a letter, or a sit-down. I always made 100 percent sure that when I approached someone about a concern, that I had my ducks in a row and there was nothing left to subjectivity. I came in with hardcore examples.

Benjamin, an executive in the financial services industry, offers this perspective. "Some barriers you address head-on. Some you try to learn the game and finesse and politic your way around them. Each situation requires a unique approach." Hawk, an executive in the health care industry, noted that "I forced myself to be comfortable in uncomfortable environments and situations. I created relationships and these are the things

I did well. Just because people are different doesn't mean you can't learn from them." According to Mongoose, an executive in the higher education industry, "As a young person, before I became an executive, I could shoot that temper pretty quick. I learned how to muzzle that and to channel that energy into very positive ways of doing things."

Making Them Feel Comfortable With Me

Several of the executives said they overcame barriers by *making others feel comfortable around them*. Derrick, an executive in the financial services industry, described it this way:

> At the end of the day, people want to be comfortable around the people that they're going to rely on to get the work done. You may know that the African American on your team has a great track record of getting things done. But, if you've never had a beer together, if you've never really had more than a "Hey. How are you doing? How's the family?" conversation, then it's hard. What I've learned over time is it's important for you to share something for the purpose of increasing the comfort level.
>
> Twenty years ago, my current boss and I didn't have a relationship and a rapport. It was pretty transactional. But, then I started talking about some things that I had learned about him. And that broke the ice. All of a sudden, his whole demeanor changed. Now, 20 years later, he's the CEO and he came to me and said, "I want this role for you." That was him taking a bet based on his comfort.

Lee, an executive in the health care industry, simply said, "I dress very, very conservatively as not to raise eyebrows." Similarly, Ranger, also an executive in the health care industry, spoke about the impact of making others comfortable around him—even when he could not identify with the situation. He said:

> Early on, I would internalize. I would laugh when things weren't funny. Early on, I started customizing my soul—for a lack of a better word. So, the way I overcame those barriers was when I started

seeing things that I perceived to not be right, I would ask questions to seek understanding.

This chapter captures the lived experiences of the 30 African American male executives who participated in this research. Although their journeys are unique to each of them, there are shared experiences among them. For example, in describing their leadership experiences, the overwhelming majority talked candidly about the barriers of bias, racism, and discrimination. They also discussed constantly feeling lonely and alone in settings of people who do not look like them. The executives also discussed their collective desire to have more mentors, sponsors, coaches, and allies as a part of their leadership journeys. Many of them talked about seeing their White counterparts have leaders champion their careers and wondered why they were not having the same experience. The executives also shared their desire to have less race, racism, conscious, and unconscious biases in their leadership journeys. In addition, they also discussed their desire to not be misunderstood as African American men by others. The executives talked about the importance of their faith, family, friends, fraternities, and other networks in providing critical support for dealing with the barriers in their leadership journeys. The next chapter builds on the lived experiences of the 30 African American male executives to explore the impact of the gap of African American male executives to U.S. corporations.

CHAPTER 4

The Impact of the Gap of African American Male Executives to U.S. Corporations

Another key area explored in this research was the impact of the gap in African American male executives in U.S. corporations to those businesses. To understand the impact of this gap, I started by asking the executives how they view the gap in the number of African American male executives in U.S. corporations. In the opinions of 29 of the 30 executives, U.S. corporations are at a competitive disadvantage without African American male and female executives. To them, the absence of African American executives could signal there were limits on advancement opportunities for diverse top talent. They also viewed the absence of African American executives as a signal that there was limited diverse representation on corporate boards that govern U.S. corporations—particularly those that are publicly traded. In addition, they viewed the absence of African Americans in U.S. corporations as an invitation for consumer backlash, which has been known to occur when consumers discover that the corporations they support financially do not have diverse representation at all levels reflecting all consumers. Here are their thoughts.

Q6: Are You Aware of the Gap in the Number of African American Male Executives in U.S. Corporations?

Awareness of the Gap

Of the 30 executives who participated in this study, 29 were aware of the gap in the number of African American male executives in U.S.

corporations. One executive was not aware of the gap. According to Lee, an executive in the health care industry, "I am not aware that a gap exists." He goes on to describe his experiences when he attends two national professional association meetings:

> I see us in that arena. There are a lot of my kind with these two groups, and I see executives. So, because I'm surrounded so often with them, I don't go around and count. I know that there's many, many of us in those circles.

When asked if he was aware of whether there is a gap for African American male executives outside of his profession, Lee said, "Can I tell you my worries don't even go that far. And maybe it should."

By comparison, the other 29 executives acknowledged their awareness of the gap. As examples, Ron, an executive in the financial services industry, said, "Yes! I'm fully aware. Living it." Vince, an executive in the health care industry, said, "Oh absolutely! It's talked about all the time." Similarly, Al, an executive in the financial services industry, said, "Oh yes. It's too visible to not be aware of it." Derrick, also an executive in the financial services industry, said, "Without a doubt. I see the gap." Bob, an executive in the health care industry, said, "Yes. I am fully aware. I like to describe us as unicorns. In some cases, you may see a unicorn before you see a Black executive."

Along these same lines, Mac, an executive in the human services industry, said, "I am well aware. You can determine that by the community in which you live and how many senior executives are there. You can tell by what's going on around the nation. So, yes. I'm definitely aware of it." John, an executive in the automobile manufacturing industry, said:

> When I can count on one hand the number of peers in the industry, and maybe count on two hands the number of peers in my service region, my geographic region, I can see pretty evidently that there's a gap.

William, an executive in the financial services industry, said:

> Very much so. The reality is we only have four Black CEOs in the Fortune 500 and, probably 10 years ago, we had maybe 10. If you

look at corporate America in general, especially now as you see all of these big companies making pledges and commitments to increase the number or percentage of Black leaders, the fact that they're even doing that is a clear sign that obviously the numbers are not there.

Hawk, an executive in the health care industry, emphatically stated:

Absolutely. Absolutely. I mean absolutely! This journey has not been one where I've been able to enjoy the ride—particularly in the car that I'm riding in. There are few people that looked like me and who shared similar cultural and ethnic backgrounds.

Tony, an executive in the financial services industry, said:

Having worked for three Fortune 500 companies and having always been in a leadership capacity at each of them, it's very visible that there was a lack or a gap in the number or ratios of African American males, in particular, in those ranks.

Blake, an executive in the higher education industry, offered these thoughts:

Yes. I am aware and let me tell you how I view it. We have been systematically excluded from growth. There has not been, outside of a few circles, that genuine interest in being inclusive, or, actually taking those efforts to pave the way for people's road to the C-suite or to executive positions.

Q7: What Problem or Challenge, If Any, Does the Gap in the Number of African American Male Executives Have on U.S. Corporations?

The following section discusses the participants' views on what problem or challenge, if any, does the gap in the number of African American male executives have on U.S. corporations.

Gap Leads to Competitive Disadvantage

A significant number of the executives believe that corporations are at a competitive disadvantage when they do not have African American male executives in decision-making roles. They also acknowledge that this gap creates a lack of diversity within organizations. According to William, an executive in the financial services industry:

> It is a proven fact that companies that are diverse, that have diverse leadership teams, outperform companies that do not. Diversity of thought, diversity of experiences, is critical. I also think that companies perform to meet the needs of their customer base. The customer is changing—the demographic, the face, the age. By not having a diverse leadership team, you're putting yourself at a competitive disadvantage. You're also probably putting a target on your back in terms of what your core values are and what you're going to ultimately be able to do as a company in terms of driving growth in the future.

According to Andrew, an executive in the commercial real estate industry:

> When you're looking to solve challenges and problems, you want to have different perspectives and points of view. So, individuals from different backgrounds and who don't fit that narrow profile bring that additional perspective and point of view to the table. And, having diversity in those leadership roles—in those conversations—is a business issue. It's not a social issue. It's no longer nice to have. It's a need to have.

According to Al, an executive in the financial services industry, "They're (corporate executives) not dealing with full information. They just don't have access to the full body of knowledge that would be available to them. I'm not sure that folks really appreciate that."

According to T.H., an executive in the advertising, marketing, and digital communications industry:

> Definitely there's a problem and it creates limitations on their ability to serve their client base. Ultimately what's going to

happen is you're limiting your talent pool, if the best talent can't rise to the top and lead. And, even to the middle. We're not all set out to be CEOs. But, we're set out to be vice presidents. Some of us are set out to be directors. Some of us are more suited for a frontline manager. But, anytime you limit talent, you're limiting the ability for your company to serve and deliver its most innovative and impactful product or service. Also, it's going to limit your sales. It's going to limit your quality of service. And, then you also limit your community.

According to Green, an executive in the environmental law industry:

Think of the solutions to a problem that a company comes up with that are short-sighted and narrow-minded because they only consult a group that thinks alike and does not think of other solutions and other approaches to a problem. I believe the companies that miss diversity are going to miss out on competition. The first company in any industry that gets in on diversity will have a competitive advantage.

According to Joshua, an executive in the health care industry:

The United States of America is becoming more diverse, becoming more brown and Black. And, so are the consumers of technology, health care, of any industry. Sometimes, the assumption is people of color don't have money. There's a lot of people of color that I know that have money. And, their purchasing power is getting bigger and bigger. And, so, those Fortune 500 or Fortune 1000 companies have to understand the urgent nature of getting people of color to help advance that opportunity within their organizations.

According to Joseph, an executive in the consumer products industry:

We have to look like our consumers, especially in these days and times. Companies are getting a lot more pressure to make sure that they have a diverse workforce and a diverse workforce at the leadership level. I think corporate America gets that. Maybe they'll come along dragging and screaming. But, they get the business reason to have diversity at senior leadership. This world is only getting darker and darker not whiter and whiter. So, they need that perspective in the boardroom as they make those decisions.

According to Ranger, an executive in the health care industry, "They're not getting the full perspective of what African Americans could bring in terms of experiences, different ways of connecting—that drive, that tenacity—just the spirit." For Tony, an executive in the financial services industry:

> To not have an environment or culture that embraces inclusion and diversity, there's a tendency for you to lose touch with your population at large and the spending power of those who are different in ethnicity and gender. That happens when you're not tapping into the creative perspective of those who are different and understanding how that can be applied to your bottom line. The spending power alone of these groups is very impactful to a company's bottom line.

Lack of Diversity in Leadership

A significant number of the participants believe that having a gap in the number of African American male executives impacts diversity across all levels of U.S. corporations. According to Chad, an executive in the health care industry, "I do strongly believe that if you have a predominately African American, Hispanic, Asian community, you need to have someone in a leadership role that represents that socioeconomic demographic." Similarly, Hawk, an executive in the health care industry, said, "America is missing out from being truly great by not having more African Americans in leadership roles in every sector and industry." According to James, an executive in the hospitality industry:

> Given the overarching shifts in demographics, this browning of America that's been taking place over the last three, four

decades—that will continue to take place. You're going to find yourself, or organizations that lack representation, will find themselves really void of enough talent to fill critical roles in the future. The math is just not going to work if you haven't already begun to identify, cultivate, and encourage men of color—African American executives—into your organization.

According to John, an executive in the automobile manufacturing industry:

Typically for the current generation of employees, the ones who just have come on board in the past five years and are coming aboard in the next 10 years or so, they're entering the workforce with certain expectations about how their workplace should mirror what they think society should be. And, they're judging companies accordingly. So, if you come across as a company that is exclusive and doesn't value talent—regardless of what it looks like—or not perceived as being inclusive and open to talent, then talented people of this particular generation will view you as a deficient employer and they'll go elsewhere because you don't fit their model.

According to Benjamin, an executive in the financial services industry:

It provides a lack of diversity and perspective, depending on the business, and the ability to reach a certain segment of your customer or client base. By overlooking talent, you're overlooking capabilities. That's going to reduce your effectiveness of grooming African American male talent.

According to Abram, an executive in the aerospace and defense industry:

We're never going to move the needle on diversity without addressing the equality issue. And, if we don't have people of color, if we don't have women, if we don't have people with disabilities, veterans, if we don't have them in the board room and around the executive table, the problem's not going to get fixed. We're all in a war for talent. And, I think that people are starting to understand that talent is pretty much evenly distributed across all lines of race and gender, but opportunity is not equal.

Limits Top Talent for Various Roles

The participants agreed that the gap in African American male executives in U.S. corporations limits top talent that is available for various roles. According to Mac, an executive in the human services industry:

> There are plenty of African American men who are qualified and equipped to hold senior-level positions within organizations. But, what I have found is that when it comes time for promotion, people tend to want to promote or support the advancement of people they have more commonality with or they have better relationships with.
>
> A lot of guys find themselves out on the golf course or having cookouts with their families, taking vacations. That doesn't always happen to us. So, if I'm the CEO, am I going to choose the person I know? Or, am I going to choose Mac who I don't know in the office but seems okay? It's usually never fair because not only did Mac not get to communicate why he was the best candidate for the job, he never even got to the table for the interview. We don't even get a chance.

According to Todd, an executive in the health care industry:

> It restricts the hope of employees that they've spent so much money recruiting to come into their organization. So now when those new employees look up and they don't see people that look like them at the top, it makes them question if they're able to achieve it.

According to Andrew, an executive in the commercial real estate industry:

> As they're looking to potentially join (an organization), top talent looks up the chain and says, "Does anybody at those leadership levels look like me?" That's part of their decision-making process on whether they'll join the organization. You walk in and you're waiting in the lobby. And, you see pictures on the wall of either current or past leaders, or when you look online and do your research, oftentimes those pictures are very homogenous and don't include you.

According to Ron, an executive in the financial services industry:

> They (corporate executives) don't realize that they're losing talent that could help them because they have a narrower view on talent. They don't realize that there are customer segments and business opportunities they might not be fully maximizing. They don't realize that it's an asset that they could be leveraging. Some of them are blind to it. They don't believe they're missing out on business opportunities. They think they have it under control and don't realize that if they have some different perspective, they might be able to do what they're doing plus more.

Limits Representation on Corporate Boards

The participants agreed that the gap in African American male executives in U.S. corporations correlates to the relative low number of African American male executives and the relative low number of African American male executives who serve on for-profit governing boards. According to Green, an executive in the environmental law industry, "Think about all of the Fortune 1000 companies that have no Black members of their boards of directors. That's a shame—a missed opportunity. Think about the companies that have few, if any, Black executives." Michael, an executive in the postsecondary education industry, said:

> We have a very small number of the same people who are African American and who serve on corporate boards. This holds true for people in leadership positions. There are other qualified African Americans. They're just not given the opportunity. So, it takes an enlightened leader to make those decisions and to give those positions to African Americans.

Invites Consumer Backlash

The participants agreed that the gap in African American male executives in U.S. corporations limits top talent and invites consumer backlash. More specifically, the executives believed that African American consumers, in particular, are aware of the impact they can have when they ban together against companies that are, in their opinions, not aware of the important nuances that distinguish their different consumers. This lack of awareness, according to some executives, can be detrimental to some corporations. According to James, an executive in the hospitality industry:

> I think there's probably going to be some financial backlash as the African American community and, most recently, the White community have become activated against some of the obvious disparities in life that exists between African Americans and non-African Americans and, specifically, African American males and some of the systemic barriers and issues that have afflicted this population for a long time. I think corporations that don't demonstrate a commitment and support to that population through their actions will end up on the wrong side of consumer decisions and consumer behaviors around where they invest their dollars.

According to Michael, an executive in the postsecondary education industry:

> It creates significant problems. It impacts not just the moment that we're in right now with Black Lives Matter. It impacts all of

our current social unrest. I like to call it restlessness. It's been going on for quite a while. People see it. Leaders see it. But, they don't think that it's as important until people begin to make demands as they are right now.

Q8: What Role, If Any, Do You Play in Closing the Gap?

Mentor/Coach/Sponsor/Ally

The 29 executives who acknowledge there is a gap in the number of African American males in U.S. corporations also acknowledge and embrace the fact that they play a role in closing the gap. Specifically, there is overwhelming acknowledgment among the African American male executives that they have a role in mentoring, coaching, sponsoring, being an ally for, and advocating on behalf of the current and future generations of African American male leaders. According to Chad, an executive in the health care industry:

> It's more like mentorship—making sure the generation behind me, my kids, their friends—are given the resources that I can say I didn't know about, even though I ended up getting them, because I'm first-generation college. And, being a mentor to people that look like me to show them that if you work hard and do what you're supposed to do, then you can make it in this world.

Joseph, an executive in the consumer products industry, noted:

> You have to have a sponsor. Mentor and sponsor are two different things. The mentors give you advice, suggestions, whatever. The sponsor is someone in the room raising their hand and saying this person needs to be the next vice president and here's why. Then, you put that person in a position to showcase his skillsets so there are no doubts. You keep pounding it in. So, when they get to that point (of decision making), it's a no-brainer. People in my position have to do that.

John, an executive in the automobile manufacturing industry, further said:

> I try to sponsor and mentor Black men on their own career jour-neys. I've got several people who report to me. I'm not shy about making sure that Black men are represented in that. I'm open with my time with everyone. So, I'll have people come to my office to talk about their careers. But, I'm particularly interested—and I actually give a little more access to my calendar—to those Black men in my company who want to talk about what their careers are like, what their aspirations are. I've got an obligation to do that.

According to Derrick, an executive in the financial services industry:

> My job is to pay it forward to the younger folks who have better exposure, clearer aspirations, and a drive that they started earlier in their career to become executives. It's also to provide them insight into the unwritten rules, how to navigate corporate cultures, how to self-assess their view of themselves versus the reality, and to be an advocate and, in some cases, a sponsor for them.

Al, also an executive in the financial services industry, noted that:

> I'm always looking for opportunities to highlight people of color and make sure that they're appropriately recognized—not at the expense of someone else who's more deserving. But, I'm just mak-ing sure that everyone is getting a chance to have that kind of exposure and to get the recognition that's been available to others. Otherwise, maybe their recognition would have gone unnoticed or their contributions may have gone unnoticed.

And, Pursley, an executive in the advertising industry, said:

> I let them know the landmines, how to navigate, what might be coming. Even though I can't tell them every single thing, I try to prepare them. It's just like a father with a son. And even though

they might be 10 years away from their leadership position, they can look back at me, hopefully, and pick up some of my techniques to use to go forward. I'm trying to give them enough things on the color palette to paint their own picture.

Role Model Behavior

Several of the executives also spoke of their desire to role model many of the behaviors they admire or wish they had in their own lives. As an example, John, an executive in the automobile manufacturing industry, said:

As I tell my kids all the time, sometimes a revolutionary act is just getting up out of bed, standing up and taking a breath— particularly in this country. So, I view one of my roles in closing the gap as modeling and being present as an African American male leader in a lot of contexts and where people don't expect it. So, I will often take on roles or go places or make presentations not because I really want to do them, but simply because they need to see a Black man in a position of influence, power, and leadership. I need to represent in a very classic sense of the word. I need to represent. So, I put myself out there to show that we can be at the table, maybe even run the table and give a positive contribution.

According to William, an executive in the financial services industry:

It's critical for me to be a living example for those people within my own organization. Through my leadership within the company, the role I play representing the company and its efforts, and spending time with our Black associates throughout the company to encourage, develop, or help them grow.

T.H., an executive in the advertising, marketing, and digital communications industry, stated that:

I'm in the middle of starting a new foundation. And, I'm going to start dealing with some of those issues that came to life when

George Floyd was killed. Also, and I normally don't talk about this, but I adopted two Black children years ago when I was single. So, I was a single dad for a number of years. I wanted to have a positive impact on their lives.

Benjamin, an executive in the financial services industry, went on to note that:

> I'm the chief diversity officer. So, I have a huge role in closing the gap. I develop strategy for our company, specifically to the hiring and promotion of African American talent in our business. I develop the programs, hiring and recruiting initiatives and partnerships externally with different agencies. But just as important is my existence just being here as a leader, how I lead, how I make a concerted effort to be accessible. I also try to make sure that I see people who may be unseen by the average leader.
>
> I've found in my career that some people just need to be talked to in a way that only we can talk to people, to tell them to get their stuff together or they're not going to get another opportunity. And, I've had a couple of people who have brought their children up to me and said, "If it wasn't for this guy, I would have been fired." Those are the types of things that I'm uniquely able to do.

According to Andrew, an executive in the commercial real estate industry:

> I'm being a role model and mentoring other diverse individuals in the organization. Because there are only a few at leadership levels, we have a responsibility and an obligation to be that role model for others and help others to advance their careers.

And Flash, an executive in the health care industry, demonstrated the experience required to be a role model. He said:

> I've got this little bag right here and I've got my first job name badge in it. I keep it on my desk. There was a young man in here the other day, an African American. I said,

"Hey, I used to have your job." He said, "What are you talking about?" I said, "I used to do your job. I used to work in dietary. I did it for eight years." He said, "No you didn't." I took my name badge out to show him. I keep that badge just to prove to people that you, too, can do this hospital leadership role.

Influence Within Their Circles and Spheres

The executives interviewed were aligned that it is their responsibility to create positive change within their own circles and spheres of influence. As Ron, an executive in the financial services industry, noted:

I'm on the board of a (publicly traded) company and I'm pushing the CEO to diversify his management ranks, to diversify and keep the board diverse, to start a Black employee network, to spend more time with diverse executives in their company—not just Black but Hispanic, Asian, Indian. I'm trying to push for change.

Within my own company, I pushed our executive team and our CEO to be more open to diversity and not just hiring—but promotions and market segments, investments, and all those things. I was one of the people who helped create the Black employee network that we now have within our company. Now we also have the Executive Black Employee Network, which is meant for all Black VPs and above. I'm the executive sponsor of that.

Within my own organization, I'm pushing the leaders on my team to be more open and to have not just diverse representation but also diverse points of view. I push in all directions.

Personally, my wife and I sponsor scholarships at two universities. We try to do everything we can to make a difference.

Blake, an executive in the higher education industry who also is an attorney, said:

I think lawyers are in a unique position. We can help establish policies that are much more inclusive. This has been particularly true for lawyers in higher education where you're literally helping an institution over a period of time be instrumental in moving society forward.

Tony, an executive in the financial services industry, is focused on leadership within the enterprise. He said:

I'm in a position to have a seat at the table. I'm in a position to influence those who are in positions of influence to influence others around them to ensure we are solidifying our ranks and diversifying them enough so that it has a positive impact on the morale of the corporation. I have a voice in encouraging, if not demanding, that there is representation at various levels to ensure that we are reaching out and having that voice in the room—or seat at the table—whether it's to make us more profitable, to improve our level of engagement and contribution from others. Everyone has a part or a role in the success of our corporation.

James, an executive in the hospitality industry, pointed out that he was lucky, too:

I'm fortunate—given my own sphere of influence and the fact that I have influence and impact over hiring systems and succession planning and promotional paths and compensation administration. So, I'm able to influence in ways that ensure that there's equity and there's representation and there's a voice. I do this with any and all underrepresented groups, with the goal of having as much diversity and as much collaboration as we can have. I own those systems and, so, I can personally impact and influence results.

I also have access to resources—dollars, time, talent—of the organization that I can deploy to the community as well, with a similar focus to advocate for and improve underserved communities.

Along with influencing at the enterprise and policy levels of their organizations, there are other equally impactful ways of bringing about positive change. For example, Ranger, an executive in the health care industry, said:

> I take that (closing the gap) as a personal charge for me. I try to net-
> work with as many people, to learn about as many people, so that
> when there are opportunities (to hire), I can tap into that network.
> When I hire people for my team, I look for opportunities to put the
> position out where people can find it. There are companies that say
> nobody (diverse) applies. But, if you post in the same place that doesn't
> have diverse viewership, you're not going to get what you're looking for.

Michael, an executive in the postsecondary education industry, is focused on advocacy. He said:

> I have a list of young men and women whose names I recom-
> mend for positions. Sometimes that takes me making the search
> consult aware of individuals I believe could do the job. Then, to
> really close the deal, I make phone calls to those people who are
> going to make those decisions. Then, sometimes it's just having a
> frank conversation with someone and saying, "If you're looking
> for someone, I have some recommendations for you."

According to Derrick, an executive in the financial services industry, it is a constant process:

> I have to continue to chip away and raise awareness to decision
> makers in the company to think about how they broaden their lens
> to look for talent that they have overlooked before because it didn't
> meet a certain profile. The role I play now is trying to be that bridge
> between the decision makers and the (talent) pipeline behind me.

Joseph, an executive in the consumer products industry, stated that influencing diversity starts with a diverse slate of candidates for each role:

> I am pushing the organization to make sure that we are inten-
> tional in bringing in more diversity. So, if we're recruiting for

a particular position, let's make sure that we're spending the extra time and effort to bring in people of color. Let's make sure we're establishing relationships with HBCUs (Historically Black Colleges and Universities) or other organizations to access these pools of talent.

We have a lot of interns in our marketing organization. Every time you look around, it's the same stereotype. It's the young, blonde female with blue eyes from the local university. I know we can do better than that. In fact, I have a conference call today with my HR VP about that very thing. We have to diversify up and down, throughout the entire organization.

According to Joshua, an executive in the health care industry:

I have a big role, just like any other man of color that's in an executive role. Somebody gave you a shot—even if that person might not have looked like you. I've hired about three people of color within the organization so far. We're going to be starting a fellowship, primarily to bring in more people of color.

Al, an executive in the financial services industry, is focused on access and advocacy:

I'm having conversations with my current peer group about opening or creating access for others, and advocating for individuals in the organization. Sometimes, it looks like recognizing an intern who's been on board for a few weeks, reaching out and having a conversation, taking that individual to lunch, learning more about their makeup, giving them some tips on how they can enhance their performance. There are times when I'm in meetings and I get to hear what others say about an individual. If I can communicate that (feedback) in a professional and positive way that's helpful to them, then I will do that.

According to Blake, an executive in the higher education industry, "Whether it's fraternal, whether it's church-related, whether it's other not-for-profits, it's important to partner with them." Similarly, William, an executive in the financial services industry, said, "I partner with organizations like the Executive Leadership Council and others that are designed specifically to develop, promote, and engage leaders from the C-suite to senior levels of companies to help others."

Green, an executive in the environmental law industry, described starting a network about 15 years ago to connect young lawyers with other lawyers who could pave the way for job and career opportunities. He anticipated having 10 or 15 participants at their first meeting. Instead, close to 100 came out. The network has evolved into a group of more than 6,000 participants across the United States. Green said, "The only thing I ask them when they get something is when the time comes help someone else." Abram, an executive in the aerospace and defense industry, stressed establishing diversity as part of a corporation or organization's overall business strategy. He said, "I'm on a nonprofit board in the industry that I work. And, I've been working to add diversity and inclusion as an agenda item as a formal part of the strategy."

Closing the Gap Is a Team Sport

The executives agree that there is a role for other leaders to play in closing the gap that exist among African American men in C-suite roles. Their alignment is grounded in their own lived experiences as well as in the literature, which suggests that the leadership journey for African American male executives is, indeed, vastly different from the leadership journey for White male executives.

The 30 African American males who participated in this study reinforced this belief as they discussed, in great detail, the challenges and barriers they have faced as they have advanced throughout their corporate careers. Those challenges and barriers included everything from not fitting the already-established preconceived notions of American leaders being masculine and White,[1] to the existence of institutional racism in U.S. corporations,[2] to not having an abundance of support from mentors,

---

[1] Hoyt and Simon (2016).

[2] A. Walter, Y. Ruiz, R. Welch, C. Tourse, H. Kress, B. Morningstar, B. MacArthur, and A. Daniels. 2017. "Leadership Matters: How Hidden Biases Perpetuate Institutional Racism in Organizations," *Human Service Organizations: Management, Leadership & Governance* 41, pp. 213–221.

sponsors, role models, coaches, and allies who are invested in their long-term success.[3]

Team Sport Starts With the Most-Senior Leaders

From these findings, there is an acknowledgment that closing the leadership gap is a team sport that starts with the most-senior leaders of U.S. corporations. Specifically, there is an opportunity for the leaders of U.S. corporations to acknowledge that these challenges and barriers exist. From there, there is an opportunity for these leaders to ensure that there are sufficient policies and practices in place to reduce them. Embedded in this scenario is the opportunity for an organization's most-senior leaders to role model being transformational leaders.

According to research, transformational leaders "raise leadership to the next level."[4] They inspire followers with challenges and persuasion, "providing both meaning and understanding." Transformational leaders also are "individually considerate, providing the follower with support, mentoring, and coaching."[5] It is against this context that the most-senior leaders of U.S. corporations can champion the changes that must occur for more African American male executives to be successful in their leadership journeys.

From their positions as CEOs and other executive roles, these most-senior leaders can establish a clear vision on why it is important for their organizations to embrace diversity and inclusion at all levels, including at the top. At the same time, they can lead by example. From the perspective of the participants, leading by example includes personally committing, or recommitting, to the success of their current African American colleagues, as well as colleagues from other ethnic groups. This commitment or recommitment should produce tangible and meaningful documented

---

[3] H. Ibarra, N.M. Carter, and C. Silva. September 2010. "Why Men Still Get More Promotions Than Women." https://nbr.org/2010/09/why-men-still-get-more-promotions-than-women.

[4] B.M. Bass and R.E. Riggion. 2006. *Transformational Leadership*, 2nd ed. (New York, NY: Routlege), p. 4.

[5] Ibid., p. 5.

actions that the most-senior leader and his or her African American colleagues could agree upon. In doing so, this agreement could pave the way for a removal of the barriers and challenges faced by many African American leaders and also provide a clear path for their success.

Similarly, if there are no African Americans or other ethnic group members currently present in an organization's executive ranks, then the most-senior leaders can commit to intentionally and immediately closing those gaps by recruiting and hiring diverse top executive talent and bringing them into meaningful roles in their organizations. In addition, the most-senior leaders must ensure the necessary support for these executives that will retain them and allow them to grow and develop into successful leaders.

As these CEOs and other most-senior leaders are taking these actions, it could result in changes to an organization's policies and practices and that would ensure these new executives receive the support they need to be successful. For example, organizations can have a policy of recruiting, hiring, developing, training, promoting, and retaining a certain percentage of African American leaders at all levels. Enforcement of this policy would be tracked as a specific metrics on a company's monthly, quarterly, and annual performance scorecards. These scorecards should be linked to the organization's numerical calculations of individual ratings for all leaders and the compensation payouts (including performance bonuses) for all leaders. From here, an implication for an organization's practice would be requiring a diverse slate of candidates when hiring for all positions in an organization.

A Road Map for Closing the Gap

It is important to acknowledge that there may be leaders who are not African American who may struggle with how to convert the implications of this research into their business strategy with supporting tactics. It is against this context that I offer the following advice specifically on how these leaders can become better mentors, coaches, sponsors, and allies.

1. *Conduct a self-assessment*
   First, start with an honest assessment of yourself. Ask yourself what barriers, if any, are preventing you from being a true champion of

diversity, equity, and inclusion in your organization? As you are answering these questions, ask yourself which African American male leader's career have you helped advance lately? What did you do? Why did you do it? What were the results? Is he still on track to continue advancing his career goals?

2. *Examine your organization's data*

Second, if you have not already, pour over the data that your Human Resources team can provide about racial and gender diversity in your organization. What does this data tell you specifically about the roles African American men are playing in your organization, including your board of directors or board of trustees?

3. *Ensure that you have diversity, equity, and inclusion (DEI) leadership at the VP or above level*

Third, if your organization does not have a DEI executive who is at least at the vice president level, reports to you, and is a member of your executive team, then exercise your ability to make this important strategic business decision happen. In doing so, hire a leader whom you will openly support as he or she assesses where you currently are with a DEI strategy and provides a recommended DEI strategy that aligns with and supports your business strategy. Ensure your DEI executive has the resources needed to activate this strategy. These resources include, and are not limited to, investments in the appropriate level of staffing and funding.

4. *Champion your organization's DEI work*

Fourth, champion the work of your DEI executive as you lead by example. Do not delegate or relegate your DEI efforts to your DEI executive. Instead, develop a strategic *partnership* with your DEI executive. Rely on his or her advice and counsel just as you do the advice and counsel of your general counsel, chief financial officer, chief strategy officer, chief marketing and communications officer, and the other members of your executive team.

5. *Make DEI a daily business priority*

Finally, just as you wake up every day thinking about your organization's financial bottom line, do the same thing with your organization's DEI results. Your executive team will watch how you are prioritizing DEI. They will take their clues and ques from you.

Ensure that your colleagues know, without a doubt, that you are personally committed to the success of all of your organization's team members, including your underrepresented team members such as African American males.

It is my hope that these five leadership opportunities, policies, and practices will be woven into the fabric of all of U.S. corporations. These opportunities, policies, and practices will only become realized when an organization's most-senior leader—specifically the CEO—is committed to championing this work as a business priority.

Q9: What Advice Would You Offer to Other African American Males Who Aspire to Executive Leadership Roles?

Advice to Future African American Executives

In the spirit of closing the gap in the number of African American males in U.S. corporations, I asked each executive what advice they would offer other African American males who aspire to executive leadership roles. Their advice can serve as a roadmap for success that other aspiring African American male executives could follow. Consistent with the literature and consistent with the findings of this research, a majority of the executives acknowledged the need for mentors, coaches, sponsors, and allies. Some of the executives advised about the need to have at least two mentors, including one who is not African American, to ensure having different perspectives.

Interestingly enough, Ron, an executive in the financial services industry, offered a slightly different perspective. He said:

Everyone always wants to find mentors and find sponsors. But, the best thing you can do is to create an environment where people want to work for and with you; where you're a magnet; where people want you on their team or people want to be around you.

William, an executive in financial services, said, "Be authentic. You can't be someone else, because sooner or later the real you is going to show up and that's going to be an adjustment for some folks." Similarly, John, an executive in automobile manufacturing, advised that it is important to:

> Have a strong sense of self that is independent of what the broader society says you are capable of; a solid sense of yourself that won't depend on what the White world or the corporate world tells you or values in you.

Hawk, an executive in the health care industry, said:

> Many times we, as African Americans, tell ourselves no. We say, "they're not going to give me that job because I'm Black, or they're not going to let me do it because I don't have PhD." Let them tell you no. Don't tell yourself no.

Several of the executives advised about being intentional in developing a network of people who will provide opportunities, who will support, and who will advocate on your behalf. They also spoke of the need to have a vision for yourself and your career. Others advised about the importance of "nailing the technical skills," as expressed by Joseph, an executive in the consumer products industry, to learning as much as you can so as to not become a "one trick pony," as expressed by Derrick, an executive in financial services.

Similarly, Neil, an executive in the defense industry, said, "Take the tough assignments, the absolute toughest. Understand culture and relationships. Don't be afraid to fail but be accountable for your failures. And, don't be afraid to ask for help." Todd, an executive in the health care industry, advised about the importance of not waiting for a leadership title to lead. "Take on the leadership role," he said. For Todd, this includes leading presentations internally and externally, making recommendations that you can back up with data, showing an understanding of the key business drivers and the expected outcomes from your ideas.

This chapter explored the impact of the gap of African American male executives in U.S. corporations to those businesses. Of the 30 African American executives who participated in this research, 29 were aware of the gap in the number of African American male executives in U.S. corporations. One executive said he was not aware of the gap. For the 29 executives who were aware of the gap, they said the gap positions corporations at a competitive disadvantage when they do not have African American male executives in decision-making roles. They also acknowledged that the gap creates a lack of diversity and equity within organizations at all levels. The gap in the number of African American male executives also contributes to the lack of African American male executives on for-profit governing boards. This gap occurs because most for-profit governing board members are chosen based, in large part, on the executive roles they have held at other corporations. The African American male executives also agree that the gap limits top talent and invites consumer backlash.

The 29 executives who are aware of the gap freely admit that they play a role in closing it. This includes these executives serving as mentors, coaches, allies, and sponsors. They also understand their role in advocating on behalf of the current and future generations of African American male leaders. The executives were also aligned with their responsibility to create positive change within their own circles and spheres of influence. This includes everything from personally funding scholarships to speaking up and lobbying for their organizations to establish and enforce policies and programs that will advance the cause of their underrepresented employees.

Equally as important, the African American executives agree that they cannot do it alone. Closing the gap is a team sport that starts with the most-senior leaders in each U.S. corporation. CEO's have the unique ability to establish a clear vision on why it is important for their organization to embrace diversity, equity, and inclusion at all levels, including the top. Also included in the chapter is a five-step road map for executives to use, if they need guidance on closing the gap in the number of African American male executives in their organizations.

CHAPTER 5

Summary of Major Findings

The purpose of this qualitative research was to explore the leadership journey of African American male executives in U.S. corporations. Specifically, the goal of this research was to hear directly, through semi-structured interviews, from African American males about their leadership journeys and their perceptions regarding factors that shaped them. This research focused on the experiences of 30 African American male executives in U.S. corporations. This chapter provides a summary of the major findings from this research.

As a reminder, these executives represented a broad array of corporations and industries in both the for-profit and not-for-profit arenas. Each participant was no more than two levels below the CEO. The participants ranged from 43 to 74 years of age, with the average age being 54 years. The participants had been in executive leadership roles ranging from 3 to 26 years, with the average being 14 years. From an educational perspective, each participant earned at least a bachelor's degree. Twelve of the 30 participants also earned the master's degree; 3 of the 30 also earned the juris doctorate; and 5 of the 30 also earned the doctorate.

Building on the purpose and goal of this study, a review of the literature, coupled with findings from this study, suggests that there is racial and ethnic underrepresentation in corporate leadership roles in the United States. As a reminder, the data indicates that White men are disproportionately represented in the vast majority of all top positions of influence. This representation ranges from the presidency of colleges and universities to the U.S. Senate and boardrooms of U.S. corporations. In U.S. corporations, White men hold 95.5 percent of board chair positions compared to minority men who hold 3.9 percent.[1] In the CEO role, the next level

---

[1]   Hoyt and Simon (2016).

below the board chair position, the number of African American CEOs always has been significantly lower than the number of White CEOs. For example, in December 2019, there were only three African American CEOs in U.S. corporations.[2] An article in the *Wall Street Journal* by Chen later reported that out of the CEOs leading the top 500 companies in the United States, just 1 percent or four were African American. In this same article, it was reported that African Americans held 3 percent of executive or senior-level roles in companies with more than 100 employees.[3] More recently, a 2021 study by McKinsey & Company titled "Race in the Workplace" reported that there are only three African American CEOs in all of the Fortune 500. Given the fact that African Americans represent 12 percent of the employees in the U.S. private sector overall, the McKinsey & Company research suggested that there should be at least 60 African American CEOs leading Fortune 500 companies.[4] In 2022, however, the number of African American CEOs leading Fortune 500 companies returned to six. Those CEOs are Roz Brewer, Walgreens Boots Alliance; Thasunda Brown Duckett, TIAA; Frank Clyburn, IFF (International Flavors and Fragrances); Marvin Ellison, Lowe's Home Improvements; David Rawlinson, Quarate Retail, Inc., which includes QVC and HSN and online retailer Zulily; and Robert Reffkin, Compass real estate.[5]

Alignment of Findings With Central Research Question and Interview Questions

Building on this data as a foundation, the central research question for this research was what is the leadership journey of African American male executives in U.S. corporations. The following interview questions were used to understand more about this central research question from the lived experiences of each executive:

1. What has your leadership journey been like?
2. What would you like to have more of in your leadership journey?

---

[2] Brooks (2019).

[3] Chen (2020).

[4] McKinsey & Company (2021).

[5] McGlaufin (2022).

3. What would you like to have less of in your leadership journey?
4. What barriers, if any, impacted your leadership journey?
5. If you had any barriers, how did you handle them?
6. Are you aware there is a gap in the number of African American male executives in U.S. corporations?
7. What problem or challenge, if any, does this gap have on U.S. corporations?
8. What role do you play, if any, in closing the gap?
9. What advice do you offer to other African American males who aspire to executive leadership roles?

Summary of Executives' Leadership Journeys

As a group, the executives' experiences, based on their responses to these questions, aligned with the literature and offered additional insights into why there is a gap in the number of African American male executives in U.S. corporations. As a group, the participants also described their experiences as African American male executives as different from the experiences they observed in White male executives. More specifically, the participants believed that their experiences included barriers and challenges that were unique to them as African American male executives that they had to overcome to be successful.

In response to the question of how do African American male executives describe their leadership journey, the theme that dominated this discussion was the challenges of being an African American male. Specifically, the vast majority of the executives described their leadership journeys as being challenging. Their challenges ranged from how they were viewed in the eyes of their White counterparts, too often not getting the best assignments and opportunities, to constantly having to prove themselves as capable and competent leaders. By contrast, one executive described his leadership journey as rewarding. Several participants also said their leadership journeys were an often-lonely experience, in spite of their accomplishments. Several participants also said there were different rules for African American males that they had to figure out to be successful. Several participants also spoke about the belief that they had to be better than their White counterparts.

The executives also acknowledged that having mentors, sponsors, role models, coaches, and allies was critical to the success of most African American male executives. At the same time, mentors, sponsors, coaches, and allies have been hard to find, and hard to keep, for many of them. Even so, some of the participants specifically spoke of the benefits of having mentors, sponsors, coaches, and allies at some point during their careers. Regardless of whether they personally had mentors, sponsors, role models, coaches, and allies, each acknowledged the value of having someone to provide insight, guidance, and counsel regarding their respective career journeys. When asked what they would like to have *more* of in their leadership journey, the desire for mentors, sponsors, coaches, and allies consistently surfaced for those who did not have these experiences.

Regardless of whether they had mentors, sponsors, coaches, and allies, as a group the executives said they would like to have more opportunities to grow and develop as leaders—particularly earlier in their lives and in their careers. For several of them, there was a desire to have access and exposure to different people and different experiences earlier in their lives, as well as now. Several of the executives also shared their desire to have more peers who looked like them and could relate to their leadership journeys. In addition, a few of the executives acknowledged their own need to be more self-confident as they progressed in their leadership journeys.

In sharing what they would like to have less of in their leadership journeys, race, racism, and conscious and unconscious biases surfaced for the vast majority of the executives. This theme rose to the top, particularly as these executives discussed what they would like to have less of in their career journeys. It also was the dominant theme when the executives described the barriers that impacted their leadership journeys. In addition, the executives also said they would like to have less of being misunderstood as an African American man. This sentiment included the misunderstandings that result from their physical statures, to how they react to certain situations, and to the emotional strain of living in multiple worlds.

In describing their leadership journeys, and specifically, any barriers that may have impacted them, the overwhelming majority of the executives said, again, that they had to deal with race and racism. For them, race and racism emerged in everything from how their leaders, peers, and team members viewed them to their ability to lead successfully in environments that were designed by White males for the success of White males. The executives said they overcame their barriers by tapping into their faith, families, friends, fraternities, and other organizations and networks. These groups provided critical support for the participants while dealing with barriers in their leadership journeys. In addition, several of the executives spoke of overcoming barriers by anticipating challenges, being self-confident, and handling challenging situations head-on. Several of the executives said they overcame barriers by making others feel comfortable around them. To this point, several of the executives spoke about how, generally speaking, the burden of proof is on them to make their White counterparts feel comfortable around them—not the other way around. They shared examples of making others feel comfortable around them, including initiating lighthearted conversation so that their White counterparts got to know more about them personally, to dressing conservatively, to laughing at jokes that may not be funny to the African American executives, or participating in conversations on topics that were relevant in the White culture but were not relevant in the African American culture.

Another way that many African Americans make others feel comfortable around them is a phenomenon known as "code-switching." Code-switching, also known as playing the part, occurs when African Americans abandon the communication styles of their culture and adapt those associated with the dominant European culture.[6] Depending on when and where code-switching occurs (business settings versus family/friend settings), those who are code-switching can be called out as being fake or not true to their culture.

---

[6] C. Nilep. 2006. "Code Switching in Sociocultural Linguistics," *Colorado Research in Linguistics* 19, pp. 1–22; M.P. Orbe. 1994. "Remember, It's Always Whites' Ball: Descriptions of African American Male Communication," *Communication Quarterly* 42, pp. 287–300.

Summary of Executives' Views of Gap in African American Males in the C-Suite

As it pertains to how do African American male executives view the gap in the number of African American male executives in U.S. corporations, the overwhelming majority of the participants acknowledged and voiced that there is a gap. Specifically, of the 30 executives who participated in this study, 29 were aware of the gap in the number of African American male executives in U.S. corporations. One executive was not aware of the gap. "I am not aware that a gap exists," said Lee, an executive in the health care industry. He went on to describe his experiences when he attends two national professional association meetings. "I see us in that arena. There are a lot of my kind in these two groups, and I see executives. I know that there's many, many of us in those circles." When asked by this researcher if he was aware of whether there is a gap for African American male executives outside of his profession, Lee said, "Can I tell you my worries don't even go that far. And maybe it should."

By comparison, for the 29 executives who acknowledged that there is a gap in the number of African American male executives in U.S. corporations, their responses to the subsequent interview questions provided insights on how they view the impact of this gap to U.S. corporations. In the opinions of the overwhelming majority of the participants, U.S. corporations are at a competitive disadvantage without African American males and other minorities in day-to-day decision-making roles. In addition, the participants also viewed the absence of African American executives as a signal that there was limited diverse representation on corporate boards that govern U.S. corporations—particularly those that are publicly traded. Beyond the executive suite, the absence of those executives also signaled to the participants that there likely are limits on the organization's ability to recruit, retain, develop, and promote diverse top talent across all levels of U.S. corporations. McGinn and Milkman go so far as to suggest that it will remain a challenge for nondiverse organizations to become inclusive as long as its decision makers, including hiring leaders, continue hiring, evaluating, sponsoring, and promoting people who look like them and with whom they are most comfortable.[7]

---

[7]   McGinn and Milkman (2013).

Besides a lack of ability to recruit the best people regardless of race, the participants also discussed how the absence of African American employees and executives in U.S. corporations could be an invitation for consumer backlash. According to many of these executives, this backlash has been known to occur when consumers discover that the corporations they support financially do not have diverse representation at all levels reflecting all consumers. The executives believed that African American consumers are more aware of the impact they can have when they ban together against companies that are, in their opinions, not aware of the important nuances that distinguish their different consumers. This lack of awareness, according to some executives, could be detrimental to some corporations. One participant offered as an example what has happened in the National Football League (NFL) starting with former football quarterback Colin Kaepernick's decision to kneel during the playing of the national anthem, to show his concern about the increase in policy brutality among African Americans and other examples of racial inequality in the United States. In this executive's opinion, because the NFL lacks African American executives in decision-making positions, the NFL mishandled leading through this situation from the beginning. As a result, many other players and fans joined Kaepernick, while others remained neutral or took the opposite stand. This gap caused a national display of disunity among players, executives, fans, and sponsors. It also damaged the reputation and the brand of the NFL.

Summary of the Executives' Views on Their Roles in Closing the Gap

Finally, there was an overwhelming consensus among the African American male executives that they had—and continue to have a role in closing the gap. For them, closing the gap included mentoring, coaching, and sponsoring others; and being allies and advocates for current and future generations of African American male leaders. To illustrate this point, John, an executive in the automobile manufacturing industry, said, "I try to sponsor and mentor Black men on their own career journeys. I've got an obligation to do that." Similarly, Chad, an executive in the health care industry, said, "It's more like mentorship—making sure the generation behind me, my kids, their friends—are given the resources that I can say I didn't know about." Pursley, an executive in the advertising industry, said, "I let them know the landmines, how to navigate, what might be coming. Even though I can't tell them every single thing, I try to prepare them. I'm just like a father with a son." Several of the executives also spoke of their desire to role model many of the behaviors they admire or wish they had in their own lives.

The executives are also aligned on their responsibility to create positive change within their own circles and spheres of influence. As an example, Ron, an executive in the financial services industry, said, "I'm on the board of a (publicly traded) company and I'm pushing the CEO to diversify his management ranks, to diversify and keep the board diverse, to spend more time with diverse executives in their company." Along these same lines, Tony, an executive in the financial services industry, said, "I'm in a position to influence those who are in positions of influence to ensure that we are solidifying our ranks and diversifying them."

Connecting Our Shared Experiences

As an African American male executive, I can very much relate to other aspects of the journeys of the executives who participated in this research. For example, I know what it's like to want a mentor. I had two true mentors very early in my corporate experience. They were African American men who spent time explaining how to understand and navigate the nuances of corporate American as a man of color. They shared their own stories of the challenges and frustrations of being undercompensated for what they did and overlooked for promotions and other advancement opportunities. They also provided guidance on how to position myself more broadly and strategically to avoid being labeled as only capable of doing "minority affairs" related communication work. Sadly, both of these mentors passed away many years ago. So, for the vast majority of my career, I have not had a mentor. Like some of the executives, I have had coaches along the way. I have been blessed with good bosses who have acknowledged my potential and have provided me with opportunities to grow and develop. Fortunately, I have had sponsors throughout my career. My sponsors ranged from bosses who advocated for me when it was time to assign ratings and determine promotions to other colleagues to superiors who were not afraid to speak up on my behalf as a strategic thought partner who can motivate and inspire people to generate results.

I, too, have experienced racism and microaggressions in various forms throughout my career. I have been in meetings when my comments appeared to fall on deaf ears with no response to what I said. I have been in settings when I walked into the room and spoke, and no one acknowledged me. I have been in meetings when assumptions were voiced about perceived limitations of my skills, or those of my team members, were openly discussed by a White colleague. I know what it is like to be at a business lunch or dinner and the waiter brings the check to a White team member, assuming that he is the highest-ranking person and is picking up the check. At the same time, I also have experienced many times when my voice was heard, and my thoughts were appreciated by colleagues. I also have experienced words of support, encouragement, and praise from colleagues for the strategic work that my team and I do on behalf of our organization.

I also know from my personal experiences as an African American male executive at a U.S. corporation what code-switching is. It happens to me on a daily basis. Depending on my audience, almost without thinking, I adjust what I say and how I say it. I pay far more attention to ensuring that my oral and written communications conform to the dominant European culture while at work or while carrying out business functions than I do while at home interacting with family and friends. If this is my experience, I would be surprised if it is not the experience of the 30 executives who participated in this study.

Like the majority of the executives who were interviewed for this book, my journey has been a blend of highs and lows, ups and downs. And, like the executives interviewed for this book, I embrace all of my experiences. They are at the heart of who I am today.

A key learning for me over the years and, in particular, over the past year as social unrest has returned to center stage, is that wherever I am leading, it is my duty to speak on behalf of those at all levels who aspire to be successful. I have come to realize and to embrace the fact that keeping my opinions and points of view to myself will not bring about change. In fact, the very opposite will happen. Most likely, things will remain the same. As a leader, and now as a scholar in leadership studies, it is my duty to advocate for those who cannot advocate for themselves.

Reflections

I am honored beyond measure to have had the opportunity to hear from 30 African American male executives about their leadership journeys in U.S. corporations. Despite their different industries, locations, and ages, the tie that bound them together was their various experiences as African American male executives. Their individual stories provided keen insight into their collective experiences. While each of them acknowledged that they have been blessed to have accomplished a lot, they also acknowledged that their accomplishments were not easy.

As I interviewed each executive and listened to his story, it gave me an opportunity to tap into my skills as a former young newspaper reporter. During my brief time as a reporter, my job always was to ask the questions in a neutral and unbiased way, and then to allow the other person to share his thoughts and perspectives. This skill served me well in conducting these interviews since I, too, am an African American male executive in a U.S. corporation. Even though I also could relate to many of the experiences these executives shared, I always knew this research was not about me.

For this reason, I always reminded myself at the beginning of each interview that my job was to ask the questions and then to accurately record their responses. My job was not to make myself a part of this research. Instead, my job was to bring to life, using their own words, the nuances of the leadership journeys of each African American male executive who participated in this study. This keen awareness of my role allowed me to interview, record, analyze, and share the results of this qualitative research study as it is presented in this research.

My hope and prayer is that the stories shared by each of these executives that are reflected in this study are an accurate tapestry of their personal journeys. I also hope and pray that the chronicling of their stories—along with the implications for leadership, policy, and practice—will pave the way for more enriching and rewarding experiences for the next generation of African American males who aspire for executive leadership roles in

U.S. corporations. These future executives will only be as successful as the encouragement and support they receive from other C-suite executives who are willing to leave the door open and invite these leaders to come in and take the seat that they have earned at the leadership table.

References

ASJE Higher Education Report. 2015. *Systemic Racism in Higher Education*. New York, NY: Wiley.

Bass, B.M. 2008. *The Bass Handbook of Leadership, Theory, Research & Managerial Applications*. 4th ed. New York, NY: Free Press.

Bass, B.M. and R.E. Riggion. 2006. *Transformational Leadership*. 2nd ed. New York, NY: Routlege.

Bouie, J. March 30, 2011. "The Segregated Workplace." *The American Prospect*. https://prospect.org/departments/segregated-workplace/.

Brooks, K.J. December 10, 2019. "Why so Many Black Business Professionals Are Missing From the C-Suite?" https://cbsnews.com/news/black-professionals-hold-only-3-percent-of-executive jobs-1-percent-of-ceo-jobs-at-fortune-500-firms-new-report-says/.

Brooms, D.R. 2017. *Being Black, Being Male on Campus: Understanding and Confronting Black Male Collegiate Experiences*. Albany: State University of New York Press.

Brooms, D.R. and A.R. Perry. 2016. "It's Simply Because We're Black Men: Black Men's Experiences and Responses to the Killing of Black Men." *Journal of Men's Studies* 24, pp. 166–184. https://doi.org/10.1177/1060826516641105.

Brown, A.L. 2011. "Same Old Stories: The Black Male in Social Science and Educational Literature, 1930s to the Present." *Teachers College Record* 113, pp. 2047–2079.

Browne, I. and I. Kennelly. 1999. "Stereotypes and Realities: Images of Black Women in the Labor Market." *Latinas and African American Women at Work: Race, Gender, and Economic Inequality*. New York, NY: Russell Sage Foundation.

Calasanti, T. and J.W. Smith. 1998. "A Critical Evaluation of the Experiences of Women and Minority Faculty. Some Implications for Occupational Research." *Current Research on Occupations and Professions* 35, pp. 239–258. Greenwich, CT: JAI Press.

Chen, T. September 28, 2020. "Why Are There Still so Few Black CEOs?" *The Wall Street Journal*. www.wsj.com/articles/why-are-there-still-so-few-black-ceos-11601302601.

Clayton, D.M., S.E. Moore, and S.D. Jones-Eversley. 2019. "The Impact of Donald Trump's Presidency on the Well-Being of African Americans." *Journal of Black Studies* 50, pp. 707–730.

Cobbs, P.M. and J.L. Turnock. 2003. "Cracking the Corporate Code: The Revealing Success Stories of 32 African American Executives." New York, NY: American Management Association.

Collins, P.H. 2004. *Black Sexual Politics: African Americans, Gender, and the New Racism*. New York, NY: Routledge Press.

Collins, S.M. 1997. "Black Mobility in White Corporations. Up the Corporate Ladder but Out on a Limb." *Social Problems* 44, pp. 55–67.

Cook, A. and C.M. Glass. 2014. "Analyzing Promotions of Racial/Ethnic Minority CEOs." *Journal of Managerial Psychology* 35, pp. 440–454.

Cornileus, T.H. 2013. "I'm a Black Man and I'm Doing This Job Very Well: How African American Professional Men Negotiate the Impact of Racism on Their Career Development." *Journal of African American Studies* 17, pp. 444–454.

Cornileus, T.H. 2016. "The Brotherhood in Corporate America." *New Directions for Adult and Continuing Education,* pp. 83–96. https://doi.org/10.1002/ace.20188.

Creswell, J.W. 2012. *Educational Research: Planning, Conducting and Evaluating Quantitative and Qualitative Research*. 4th ed. Boston, MA: Pearson.

Curry, J.T. 2017. *The Man-Not: Race, Class, Genre, and the Dilemmas of Black Manhood*. Philadelphia, PA: Temple University Press.

Dixon, T.J. 2006. "Psychological Reactions to Crime News Portrayals of Black Criminals: Understanding the Moderating Roles of Prior News Viewing and Stereotype Endorsement." *Communication Monographs* 73, pp. 162–187. https://doi.org/10.1080/03637500600690643.

Dixon, T.J. 2007. "Black Criminals and White Officers: The Effects of Racially Misrepresenting Law Breakers and Law Defenders on Television News." *Media Psychology* 10, pp. 270–291. https://doi.org/10.1080/15213260701375660.

Dixon, T.J. 2008. "Crime News and Racialized Beliefs: Understanding the Relationship Between Local News Viewing and Perceptions of African Americans and Crime." *Journal of Communication* 58, pp. 106–125. https://doi.org/10.1111/j.1460-2466.2007.00376.x.

Dixon, T.J. 2017. *A Dangerous Distortion of Our Families: Representations of Families, by Race, in News and Opinion Media*. https://s3.amazonaws.com/coc-dangerousdisrution/full-report.pdf.

Dixon, T.L. and D. Linz. 2000. "Overrepresentation and Underrepresentation of African Americans and Latinos as Lawbreakers on Television News." *Journal of Communication* 50, pp. 131–154.

Entman, R.M. 1992. "Blacks in the News: Television, Modern Racism and Cultural Change." *Journalism & Mass Communication Quarterly* 69, pp. 341–361. https://doi.org/10.1177/1077-69909206900209.

Entman, R.M. 1994. "Representation and Reality in the Portrayal of Blacks on Network Television News." *Journalism & Mass Communication Quarterly* 71, pp. 509–520. https://doi.org/10.1177/107769909407100303.

Entman, R.M. and A. Rojecki. 2000. *The Black Image in the White Mind: Media and Race in America.* Chicago, IL: The University of Chicago Press.

Feagin, J. and K. Ducey. 2019. *Racist America: Roots, Current Realities, and Future Reparations.* 4th ed. New York, NY: Routledge.

Frazier, E.F. 1939. *The Negro Family in the United States.* Chicago, IL: University of Chicago Press.

Fuller, A.A. 2004. "What Difference Does Difference Make? Women, Race-Ethnicity, Social Class, and Social Change." *Race, Gender & Class* 11, pp. 1–18.

Gilens, M. 1999. *Why Americans Hate Welfare.* Chicago, IL: University of Chicago.

Goldstein, D.M. and K. Hall. 2017. "Postelection Surrealism and Nostalgic Racism in the Hands of Donald Trump." *Journal of Ethnographic Theory* 7, pp. 379–406.

Grodsky, E. and D. Pager. 2001. "The Structure of Disadvantage: Individual and Occupational Determinants of the Black-White Wage Gap." *American Sociological Review* 66, pp. 542–567.

Gündemir, S., A.C. Homan, C.K.W. de Dreu, and M.V. Vugt. 2014. "Think Leader, Think White? Capturing and Weakening an Implicit Pro-White Leadership Bias." *PLoS One* 9. http://dx.doi.org.ncat.idm.oclc.org/10.1371/journal.pone.0083915.

Harper, S.R. 2015. "Success in These Schools? Visual Counternarratives of Young Men of Color and Urban High Schools They Attend." *Urban Education* 50, pp. 139–169. https://doi.org/10.1177/0042085915569738.

Harts, M. 2019. *The Memo: What Women of Color Need to Know to Secure a Seat at the Table.* New York, NY: Seal Press.

Hinson, W.R. 2018. "Land Gains, Land Losses: The Odyssey of African Americans Since Reconstruction." *American Journal of Economics and Sociology* 77, pp. 893–939. https://doi.org/10.1111/ajes.12233.

Howard, T.C. 2014. *Black Male(d). Peril and Promise in the Education of African American Males.* New York, NY: Teachers College Press.

Hoyt, C.L. and S. Simon. 2016. "The Role of Social Dominance Orientation and Patriotism in the Evaluation of Racial Minority and Female Leaders." *Journal of Applied Social Psychology* 46, pp. 518–528.

Hunt, L.L. and M.O. Hunt. 2001. "Race, Region and Religious Involvement: A Comparative Study of Whites and African Americans." *Social Forces* 80, pp. 605–631.

Ibarra, H., N.M. Carter, and C. Silva. September 2010. *Why Men Still Get More Promotions Than Women.* https://nbr.org/2010/09/why-men-still-get-more-promotions-than-women.

Klenke, K. 2016. *Qualitative Research in the Study of Leadership.* 2nd ed. United Kingdom: Emerald Group Publishing Limited.

Konrad, A.M. 2018. "Denial of Racism and the Trump Presidency." *Equality, Diversity and Inclusion: An International Journal* 37, pp. 14–30.

Lindlof, T.R. and B.C. Taylor. 2011. *Qualitative Communication Research Methods.* 3rd ed. Thousand Oaks, CA: SAGE.

McElroy, S.W. and L.T. Andrews, Jr. 2000. "The Black Male and the U.S. Economy." *Annals of the American Academy of Political and Social Science* 569, pp. 160–175.

McGinn, K.L. and K.L. Milkman. 2013. "Looking Up and Looking Out: Career Mobility Effects of Demographic Similarity Among Professionals." *Organization Science* 24, pp. 1041–1060.

McGlaufin, P. May 23, 2022. "The Number of Black Fortune 500 CEOs Returns to Record High—Meet 6 Chief Executives." *Fortune.* https://fortune.com/2022/05/23/meet-6-black-ceos-fortune-500-first-black-founder-to-ever-make-list/.

McKinsey & Company. 2021. *Race in the Workplace: The Black Experience in the U.S. Private Sector.* www.mckinsey.com/featured-insights/diversity-and-inclusion/race-in-the-workplace-the-black-experience-in-the-us-private-sector.

Muta, A.D. 2006. *Progressive Black Masculinities.* New York, NY: Taylor & Francis Group.

Newsome, C.D. 2013. *Upward Mobility Among African-American Male Executives in Corporate America: A Phenomenological Study* [Doctoral dissertation]. Retrieved from ProQuest database at Bluford Library at www.ncat.edu.

Nilep, C. 2006. "Code Switching in Sociocultural Linguistics." *Colorado Research in Linguistics* 19, pp. 1–22.

Ogungbure, A. 2019. "The Political Economy of Niggerdom: W.E.B. Du Bois and Martin Luther King Jr. on the Racial and Economic Discrimination of Black Males in America." *Journal of Black Studies* 50, pp. 273–297.

Orb, A., L. Eisenhauer, and D. Wynaden. 2001. "Ethics in Qualitative Research." *Journal of Nursing Scholarship* 33, pp. 93–96.

Orbe, M.P. 1994. "Remember, It's Always Whites' Ball: Descriptions of African American Male Communication." *Communication Quarterly* 42, pp. 287–300.

Ospina, S. and E. Foldy. 2009. "A Critical Review of Race and Ethnicity in the Leadership Literature: Surfacing Context, Power and the Collective Dimensions of Leadership." *The Leadership Quarterly* 20, pp. 876–896.

Parker, L. 2019. "Who Let the Dogs in? Antiblackness, Social Exclusion, and the Question of Who Is Human." *Journal of Black Studies* 50, pp. 367–387.

Parks-Yancey, R. 2006. "The Effects of Social Group Membership and Social Capital Resources on Careers." *Journal of Black Studies* 36, pp. 515–545.

Romer, D., K. Jamieson, and N.J. de Coteau. 1998. "The Treatment of Persons of Color in Local Television News: Ethnic Blame Discourse or Realistic Group Conflict?" *Communication Research* 25, pp. 268–305. https://doi.org/10.1177/009365090825003002.

Rosette, A., G.J. Leonardelli, and K.W. Phillips. 2008. "The White Standard: Racial Bias in Leader Categorization." *Journal of Applied Psychology* 93, pp. 758–777. https://doi.org/10.1037/0021-9010.93.4.758.

Rowan, G.T., E. Pernell, and T.A. Akers. 1996. "Gender Role Socialization in African American Men: A Conceptual Framework." *Journal of African American Men* 1, pp. 3–22. https://doi.org/10.1007/BF02733916.

Ryan, K., S.A. Haslam, T. Morgenroth, F. Rink, J. Stoker, and K. Peters. 2016. "Getting on Top of the Glass Cliff: Reviewing a Decade of Evidence, Explanations, and Impact." *The Leadership Quarterly* 27, pp. 446–455.

Schaffner, B.F., M. MacWilliams, and T. Nteta. 2018. "Understanding White Polarization in the 2016 Vote for President: The Sobering Role of Racism and Sexism." *Political Science Quarterly* 133, pp. 9–34.

Smith, J.W. and S.E. Joseph. 2010. "Workplace Challenges in Corporate America: Differences in Black and White." *Equality, Diversity and Inclusion: An International Journal* 29, pp. 743–765. https://doi.org/10.1108/02610 151011089500.

Smith, J.W. and T. Calasanti. 2005. "The Influences of Gender, Race and Ethnicity on Workplace Experiences of Institutional and Social Isolation: An Exploratory Study of University Faculty." *Sociological Spectrum* 25, pp. 307–334.

Smithsonian National Museum of American History. 2012. *Separate Is Not Equal. White Only: Jim Crow in America.* Washington, D.C. https://americanhistory .si.edu/brown/history/1-segregated/white-only-1.html.

Stack, D.W. 2015. *Primer of Public Relations Research.* New York, NY: The Guilford Press.

Stewart, R. 2007. *The Declining Significance of Black Male Employment: Gendered Racism of Black Men in Corporate America.* Paper presented at annual meeting of the American Sociological Association, New York.

Taylor, J.E. 2004. *The New Frontier for Black Men: A Shifting View of Senior Leaders in Organizations* [Doctoral dissertation]. San Francisco Bay, CA: Alliant International University.

Teasley, M.L., J.H. Schiele, C. Adams, and N.S. Okilwa. 2018. "Trayvon Martin: Racial Profiling, Black Male Stigma, and Social Work Practice." *Social Work* 63, pp. 37–45.

Thomas, A. and S. Sillen. 1971. *Racism and Psychiatry.* New York, NY: Carol Publishing Group.

Thomas, D.A. and J.J. Gabarro. 1999. *Breaking Through: The Making of Minority Executives in Corporate America.* Boston: Harvard Business School Press.

Tomkiewicz, J., O.C. Brenner, and T. Adeyemi-Bello. 1998. "The Impact of Perceptions and Stereotypes on the Managerial Mobility of African Americans." *The Journal of Social Psychology* 138, pp. 88–92.

Turner, C. and L. Grauerholz. 2017. "Introducing the Invisible Man: Black Male Professionals in Higher Education." *Humboldt Journal of Social Relations* 39, pp. 212–227. www.jstor.org/stable/90007881.

U.S. Bureau of Labor Statistics. 2018. "U.S. Department of Labor (2018)." *Table 1. Employed and Experienced Unemployment Persons by Detailed Occupation, Sex, Race, and Hispanic or Latino Ethnicity. Annual Average 2018 (Current Population Survey)*. Data provided via e-mail from Hao Duong, Economist, U.S. Bureau of Labor Statistics.

U.S. Bureau of Labor Statistics. 2020. "Population Estimates Program (2020)." www.census/gov/quickfacts/fact/note/US/RHI425218.

Wallington, C.F. 2020. "Barriers, Boarders, Boundaries: Exploring Why There Are so Few African-American Males in the Public Relations Profession." *Public Relations Journal* 12. https://prjournal.instituteforpr.org/.

Walter, A.W., Y. Ruiz, R. Welch, C. Tourse, H. Kress, B. Morningstar, B. MacArthur, and A. Daniels. 2017. "Leadership Matters: How Hidden Biases Perpetuate Institutional Racism in Organizations." *Human Service Organizations: Management, Leadership & Governance* 41, pp. 213–221.

Wheeless, C. 2021. *You Are Enough: Reclaiming Your Career and Your Life With Purpose, Passion, and Unapologetic Authenticity*. Herndon, VA: Amplify Publishing.

Wilcox, B., W. Wang, and R. Mincy. 2018. "Black Men Making It in America: The Engines of Economic Success for Black Men in America." Institute of Family Studies. www.issuelab.org/resource/black-men-making-it-in-america-the-engines-of-economic-success-for-black-men-in-america.html.

Wilderson, F. 2017. "Blacks and Master/Slave Relation." *Afro-Pessimism Reader*, pp. 15–30. Minneapolis, MN: Avante-Garde.

About the Author

Charles F. (Chuck) Wallington is a C-suite executive and a chief marketing and communications officer. For the past 12 years, Chuck has held leadership roles in the health care industry. Previously, he held leadership roles in the financial services and the consumer-packaged goods industries.

After a brief stint as a newspaper reporter, the University of North Carolina Journalism and Mass Communications School graduate segued into public relations and marketing where he has been blessed to enjoy a successful career. He later earned a master's in communications management from the S.I. Newhouse School of Public Communications at Syracuse University.

Chuck also earned his PhD in Leadership Studies from North Carolina A&T State University. His 2021 dissertation, *Navigating the C-Suite: Exploring the Leadership Journey of African American Male Executives in U.S. Corporations*, inspired this book.

Index

Note: Page numbers followed by t refers to tables.

Printed in the USA
CPSIA information can be obtained
at www.ICGtesting.com
LVHW020001251124
797314LV00005B/55